PRAISE FOR
MINUTE FOR MARRIAGE

Minute for Marriage is one of my top recommendations for a daily devotional to strengthen your marriage and renew your commitment to your spouse. The Harpers write in an easy-to-understand way that cuts right to the heart of common marriage difficulties while also giving you daily action steps to take your marriage to the next level.
—**Dr. Ron & Ava Bates**, Founding & Sr. Pastors, The Light Church

Romans 12:10 says, "Be devoted to one another in love. Honor one another above yourselves." This verse represents the awesome example Jon and Teresa Harper have set for us over the last twenty years. What they speak with their mouths is actually how they live. Their commitment to making their marriage last a lifetime has been an example to us. We know they only speak from their wide range of experiences as they poured their heart into this book. We believe it is a must-read for all couples looking to strengthen their marriage.
—**Greg and Mary Lea Dunn,** Evangelists

As much as I love my family, the truth is sin has made us all a little bit broken. In fact, marriage is simply one broken person marrying another broken person and having little broken children. No wonder we sometimes fight. So it is refreshing to see a new resource designed to help us fight FOR our family. Minute for Marriage is an excellent book for new couples to establish a solid relational foundation. It is a great reminder to seasoned couples of what matters most. Every couple needs a copy for themselves and a copy to give to their friends!
—**Preston Cave**, TBM Missions & Discipleship

Observing Jon and Teresa navigate a life filled with a flourishing ministry, engaged parenting, and developing leaders gave us a front-row seat in applying the gold nuggets shared in Minute for Marriage. This must-have devotional will launch marriage-building conversations that will enrich your first or many years of marriage. Relationships took a hit during COVID. We highly recommend this book to those ready to grow or reestablish the thriving marriage God has in mind for Christian couples.

—**Drs. Johnnie and Ted Seago,** Certified John Maxwell Speakers and Executive Director, Family Education Foundation; Headmaster/CFO, Paideia Classical School

THE WORD
MINISTRIES
EST. 2007

JON & TERESA HARPER

MINUTE FOR MARRIAGE

Turning Minutes
into a Marriage that Lasts a Lifetime

Jon & Teresa Harper
The WORD Ministries
PO Box 613
Willis, TX 77378
Phone: 713-417-2997   Email: jonandteresaharper@gmail.com

Book Layout © 2022 Harvest Creek Publishing & Design

Ordering Information:
Quantity sales: Special discounts are available on quantity purchases by churches, associations, and others. For details, please contact the authors at the information above.

Minute for Marriage/ Jon & Teresa Harper. -- 1st ed.
ISBN 978-1-7373567-7-6

Printed in The United States of America

TABLE OF CONTENTS

DEDICATION

This work has truly been a labor of love. It has required perseverance, time, and dedication. Therefore, we dedicate this book first to God to be used for His Glory. He is the creator of marriage and desires marriages to last a lifetime!

Next, we dedicate this work to our parents, who have given us marriage examples that we learned from and have used to shape our beliefs and values of marriage.

This book is also dedicated to our three amazing blessings from God, our children Lexi, Wade, and Dylan. You have seen the good times and the rough times in our marriage. It's our prayer that as you enter a marriage covenant, you will see that no matter what, your marriage can last a lifetime. We pray that you place Jesus at the center of your lives and homes so that you can reap the blessings of a thriving marriage.

Finally, to married couples and singles everywhere, we dedicate this book to you. You don't have to be a statistic. Your marriage doesn't have to suffer and end. You can win. Your marriage can succeed, and it is our prayer that it does—until death do you part!

FOREWORD

NO HUMAN RELATIONSHIP represents the love of our Heavenly Father more than marriage. God loves every human without condition. Loving your spouse unconditionally will portray for them the deep love of their Heavenly Father. Marriage is a high calling.

Minute for Marriage: Turning Minutes into a Marriage that Lasts a Lifetime by Jon and Teresa Harper is a treasure trove of Biblical and practical wisdom to honor Christ and love your spouse. With each page turn, you will be encouraged to drink from the endless well of Christ and will receive practical help to love your spouse deeply. Imagine the strength and encouragement of intimacy with your Heavenly Father alongside your spouse.

When I was only nineteen years old, I had the honor of being Teresa (Sodek) Harper's youth pastor. Back in the day, her stepdad used to give me his JCPenney credit card so I could buy dress clothes for church! I have watched the Harpers grow in faith, family, ministry, and marriage over the years. Jon and Teresa Harper's ministry is a life-giving, gospel-rich gift to the church.

Read a chapter. Hug your spouse. Grow in your marriage.

For the Gospel in Texas,

Jonathan L. Smith, D.Min., Director of Church Health Strategy
Texas Baptists (Baptist General Convention of Texas)

INTRODUCTION

IT SEEMS LIKE the more people we talk to, the more we hear about marriages ending in divorce or coming close to it. While we are not experts, doctors, or professional counselors, we are passionate about helping marriages thrive and last for a lifetime. That's how this book was birthed.

Minute for Marriage is written in 31 bite-sized chapters that provide principles we have used and seen others use to change marriages for the better. We believe that all the chapters can galvanize your marriage if applied. The book format is written so that you may read it daily or pick it up and dive in whenever convenient.

We encourage you to use this book as a marriage experiment by rating your marriage as it is now. Then, see where it is *after* you have read and applied the takeaways tucked into each chapter. Your marriage may be good at this point—but we want it to be great!

Perhaps you picked up this book because your marriage is on the verge of collapse. We believe that your marriage can survive and even thrive. Marriage matters, and by using *Minute for Marriage,* yours can be all you and your spouse desire it to be!

Jon & Teresa Harper

SECTION 1

THINGS NEEDED FOR A "T"-RIFFIC MARRIAGE

CHAPTER 1

TOGETHERNESS

THROUGHOUT HISTORY, tandems and teams of people have come together to accomplish great things. For example, in the world of show business, groups like Abbott and Costello, The Three Stooges, and The Marvel Avengers came together and created entertainment that has lasted for years.

Historically, groups like The Allied Forces and other armies joined to fight evil and save the world. Where would the music industry be without groups like The Beatles, The Beach Boys, and others?

The sports world has witnessed dynasties like The Chicago Bulls, The Pittsburgh Steelers, New England Patriots, Boston Celtics, New York Yankees, and other great teams combine their talents and lay their egos aside to win multiple championships. So what makes these and countless others successful? We think you would agree that their togetherness and desire to accomplish a common goal was the dominant trait.

Then this begs the question, what would happen if we applied that single-minded purpose and focused on achieving something *together* in our marriages? What if making the goal to be married until death do us part was the overarching goal and purpose that we rallied around and made that the unifying battle cry?

It's probably safe to say that the people and groups mentioned above didn't always agree. There may have been times when they didn't like each other. But despite that, they united around a common purpose to win, succeed, and make history. We can, as well. So let's put aside everything that separates us and the things that make us not like our spouses and pursue "being together forever" as our goal.

It's easy to take a stick or twig and break it. But have you ever tried to break 10 or more sticks at one time? It's virtually impossible. There truly is strength in numbers.

ONE PLUS ONE EQUALS THREE

In Genesis 2, the Bible states that the two became One flesh. Then in John 17, while in The Garden of Gethsemane, before He went to the cross to die for the sins of mankind, Jesus prayed for us to be One, to come together so that the world would know He is real and that He came to be the Savior of the world. So from these two passages, we can conclude that God desires unity, and when we come together, He blesses that.

Why? Because division is brought about by the brokenness that comes with sin. Because Jesus defeated sin and broke its bondage. The alternative to brokenness and despair is joy, peace, and blessing.

Marriage is much like this. We can easily get divided and broken by things and issues that arise. However, marriage can also be like a bundle of sticks and become unbreakable, undivided, and strong. For our marriages to become like a group of twigs, togetherness must be the overarching reality and desire. So how do we come together? How do we make togetherness the norm?

First, as people of faith, we believe God gave us our spouses. We also believe that He doesn't make mistakes. Therefore, if He doesn't make mistakes, then your marriage and your spouse aren't a mistake. Therefore, there should be nothing that would divide a perfectly united marriage created by a perfect God!

Secondly, after God, our spouses should be the most important person in our lives. This means that our feelings, the issues that divide us, and nothing else should be as important to us as our spouse! Kids, financial struggles, opinions of others, that lingering issue, that problem, whatever the situation, it is not worthy of being divided from your spouse. God always blesses unity; He never blesses division.

Finally, being "right" is not as important as being united. We all have opinions. We all feel strongly about things. The problem is that we can let the intense urge to be right cause us to assert our feelings or opinions into our marriage. We can latch on to our opinions and hold on for dear life so that the wedges of bitterness, pride, frustration, and other division-causing issues seep into our relationship and cause problems.

It boils down to one thing, PRIDE. Pride seeks self over service. It desires to be right rather than listening to the other person's side. Instead of saying, "I'm sorry," pride makes us want to hold on to what bothers us rather than making amends and coming together.

> *Being "right" is not as important as being united.*

The question is, "What's worth more to you—your pride or your marriage?" Are you willing to forgive and lay aside your own agenda and opinions to watch your marriage grow and be blessed by God?

Have you allowed bitterness or animosity to seep in due to unresolved issues? Maybe there is unforgiveness or hurt that hasn't been dealt with, and it is keeping the two of you from becoming unified.

Think about how every successful team, business, or leader has had problems and hard times arise. The focus on the end result is what propels them to endure and persevere until the goal is accomplished. Let's make unity and being in our marriages for the long haul the purpose that drives us to persist and persevere when

21

everything gets complicated. It will require sacrifice, determination, and keeping the goal in sight.

This is why the majority of marriages fail. Things get hard, situations arise, and people give in and quit rather than continuing to fight, claw, and commit to making their marriage permanent. They are saying that the problem is greater than the marriage they entered. Please understand that we are not encouraging you to stay in a dangerous relationship or one that would cause harm to anyone. But we *are* saying that your marriage can be an example of unity by committing to stay the course despite the issues you face. And we believe in a God that can heal all hurt and brokenness if we allow Him.

 — Taking a Minute for Your Marriage

Spend a moment reflecting on a time when you felt a strength that came from beyond what you and your spouse had to offer. Just like a bundle of twigs that can't be broken, have there been opportunities where you both joined with Christ to find strength in your relationship? Are there areas where you need the Lord to bind you together so your marriage can't be broken?

Has pride been tearing your marriage apart? Spend time alone or with your spouse, asking the Lord to remove these thoughts of pride so you can be united in Christ.

CHAPTER 2

TRUST

IN THE WORLD we live in today, trust is rarely seen. In most cases, few are truly "people of their word." Lying, hiding the truth, or not being trustworthy enough to share what needs to be said has created a culture where secrets and addictions have become the norm.

The media bombards us with people and characters who will lie, cheat, and steal to get what they want. Unfortunately, a lack of trust has made its way into countless marriages, ultimately leading to heartache, shame, divorce, and destruction.

Twice in Scripture, we are taught a very timely principle. First, in James 5:12 (ESV), we are told, "Above all, my brothers, do not swear, either by heaven or by earth or by any other oath, but let your 'yes' be yes and your 'no' be no, so that you may not fall under condemnation." Then, in Matthew 5:37 (ESV), Jesus says, "Let what you say be simply 'Yes 'or 'No'; anything more than this comes from evil."

These Scriptures teach us that our lives are not to be a contradiction to the words we say. Instead, we need to be people of our word who can be trusted. Why? Because the verses above teach us that evil causes a lack of trust, leading to condemnation.

Marriage should be valued and treasured by both parties so that trust becomes a way of life. For example, we each have complete

Our lives are not to be a contradiction to the words we say.

and total access to each other's phones, social media accounts, and banking information. Also, early in our marriage, we made a pact that neither of us would be alone in a room or a vehicle with someone of the opposite sex without our spouse or someone else being there. This provides accountability, protects our integrity, and fosters trust in our marriage. These parameters have helped us, and many other couples, cultivate a feeling of 100% trust and confidence in marriage.

This trust we have in each other gives us one less thing to worry about and solidifies our marriage because neither of us has to wonder or be concerned that something is going on with someone else. We also don't have to worry about pornography and its unflinching grip ruining us because of the transparency we share with one another.

Maybe your marriage is like ours, and trust is not an issue. Praise Jesus for that. But perhaps you or someone you know has a marriage riddled with uncertainty or wondering based on a lack of trust. Maybe your marriage has broken trust, and your lives are shattered. Perhaps you're trying to hold on and endure after facing the consequences of situations that allowed mistrust, dishonesty, and destruction to enter.

If one of the last two scenarios is where you find yourself, then we want you to know that there is hope. The same God that created marriage and blessed the first marriage wants to restore yours. Scripture teaches that God can't lie. It's impossible for Him to do so. Therefore, He is the personification of truth. We can run to Him and beg Him for help because He only does things consistent with who He is. He can help you find peace and trust again. He can help restore and make new what has been broken.

Your marriage is important and worth fighting for. But unfortunately, day after day, we face other challenges that come against the commitments we made to our spouse on our wedding day. So one way to show them and everyone who knows you that your commitment to your spouse is as strong today as it was when you said, "I do," is to create an atmosphere of trust. Be open. Don't hide anything.

GUARD YOURSELF AND YOUR SPOUSE

A trusting marriage is a guarded marriage. Both spouses will guard themselves individually and together as a couple. They will protect themselves against outside forces that try to tear them apart. Guys, don't give her a reason to question your integrity. Don't cause her to lose trust in you. Ladies, don't hide anything. Be forthright and honest. Talk it out when in doubt and make a mutual decision.

Being open breeds trust and honesty! Too many people worldwide are known for what they said or intended to do but never actually did. Set boundaries and remove any suspicious activity.

> *The heart of her husband trusts in her, and he will*
> *have no lack of gain.*
> PROVERBS 31:11 ESV

Though there are many ways to describe trust, we need to start with a definition. One dictionary (Houghton Mifflin) defines trustworthiness this way: "Warranting trust; reliable." It implies the concept of being sound. When we use the word "sound" in this sense, we mean whole, complete, uncorrupted, or unimpaired. It is closely related to the quality of integrity.

A piece of wood furniture that still has its integrity is in good working condition without rot or breakage. Likewise, a metal spring that still stretches and retracts has its integrity. In other words, something that retains its designed or intended quality has integrity.

With this being said, does your marriage have integrity? Can you be trusted? Are you and your spouse creating a trustworthy environment where nothing is off-limits? Is everything out in the open? If trust has been broken or is in question, can you make adjustments that promote trust in both of you? Your marriage is worth it. Your family is worth it. Your future is worth it.

So how do we do this? What's the answer? Give your spouse access to your phone, computer, and anything you consider private. Make each other aware of expenditures that you are making. Ensure that your spouse knows whom you are talking to. Do not be in a vehicle or a room with anyone of the opposite sex without someone else being present. Do not share anything with someone else that would cause you to develop feelings for them that should be reserved only for your spouse.

Finally, watch what you allow to enter your mind and heart. If certain movies, websites, TV shows, or music spawn lust and desire for someone other than our spouse, they must be eradicated. What's done in secret will come to light.

 — Taking a Minute for Your Marriage

Is trust apparent in your marriage? Do you have complete confidence in the actions and expressions of your spouse? If not, take a moment to discuss this with them and set boundaries that will create an atmosphere of trust and confidence in one another. If trust has been broken, ask God to heal that brokenness and help restore the integrity of your marriage once again.

CHAPTER 3

TALK

PEOPLE USE MANY PHRASES like "Talk is cheap" and "Actions speak louder than words." The issue is that though we often use these phrases, they aren't true in most cases. For instance, we can say talk is cheap, but our words can hurt others, especially our spouses. Yes, actions speak louder than words in the sense that what we believe is seen by what we do or don't. But sometimes, words need to be used in life and marriage to convey how we feel and bring openness and authenticity to our relationships.

In this chapter, we will dive into the concept of talk. We will explore how what we say can cripple and damage our marriages. Additionally, you'll learn how not talking about issues and things weighing heavily on us can create hostility and hurt that can lead to unwanted and unnecessary pain.

Our words reflect our hearts. Think about that for a minute. What you and I say is a direct result of our hearts.

> *For out of the abundance of the heart the mouth speaks.*
> MATTHEW 12:34B ESV

In this passage, Jesus is speaking to religious leaders and people who thought they had it all together. They looked good on the outside, but Jesus confronts them with the problem seeping out from the inside. All of us are guilty of saying things we don't mean. Many of us can probably relate to "flying off the handle" in a moment of rage and letting a volcano of anger and nastiness erupt from our lips.

In Proverbs, considered the book of wisdom, we read that the power of life and death is found in the tongue. Many of the Proverbs were written by Israel's King Solomon, who many believe was the wisest person on Earth at the time. So think about this: the man thought to be the wisest of all writes a book about wisdom containing these words.

> *Death and life are in the power of the tongue, and those who love it will eat its fruits.*
> PROVERBS 18:21 ESV

This is what law enforcement would call a "clue." If the wisest man on Earth thought it was important to monitor our words—because of the effect those words would have on others—then why do we think it's no big deal?

The truth is, in most cases, we don't think; we simply speak. We can cripple and destroy someone now and potentially their future by spewing venomous words about them to anyone who will listen. But conversely, we can use our words to edify and encourage them and propel them to believe they were created for greatness and can be and do whatever they choose.

Let's try a little experiment. If I told you that you have greatness inside of you and can accomplish anything you set your mind to, how would that make you feel? Or think about encouraging a child to believe that they can achieve anything. Then, no matter how small in stature they may be because someone told them they were capable of greatness, they became 10 feet tall and bulletproof.

The same principle holds true in our marriages. If we encourage and uplift our spouses, our marriage will be more harmonious. We will find that they desire to meet our needs, and their attitude toward us will be respectful and grateful. On the flip side, if we are constantly nagging, criticizing, barraging them with negativity, and reminding them of their shortcomings, we will see our marriages suffer from being less than the best.

SPEAKING FROM A HUSBAND'S POINT OF VIEW

When my wife tells me I've done something good or that she is proud of me, I feel like I can conquer the world. This is especially true if she notices something I have done or have put a lot of effort into. However, suppose she fails to acknowledge my efforts or comes after me in a confrontational tone, bringing up something I didn't do or doing something the way she doesn't think should be done. In that case, I get defensive, and it causes me to be angry and stand-offish. Do you encourage and speak life to your spouse, or are you critical, nagging, and discouraging, making your spouse feel defeated and empty?

Another aspect of talk that will make or break your marriage is holding things back and not sharing things that bother or hurt us. Maybe the reason is we don't feel like we have the freedom to share. But, on the other hand, perhaps it's because we think that sharing what's bothering us will only worsen matters and increase hostility and disagreements. Whatever the reason might be, the Bible gives a solution.

In James 1, we are instructed to be quick to listen, slow to speak, and slow to become angry. Imagine if we adopted this notion and applied it to our marital confrontations and conversations. Instead of always replying with a comeback or being defensive, if we actually applied what this verse instructs, we would see a breakthrough. We would become more aware of the tools our enemy Satan uses to divide and split up our marriages. Those tools would be discarded, and our marriages would be healed and unified! We must be willing to listen more, speak less, and refuse to let anger control what we say.

An old adage says, "If you don't have anything nice to say, don't say anything at all." While this phrase is typically used about *what* we say about others, we believe it can also refer to *how* we say what we say. The way we talk is just as important as what we say. Others can tell how we feel and what we mean by the tone and volume of how we speak. Maybe we should start counting to 10 and regaining composure before we talk. Perhaps we should simply walk away until we can calmly respond and share what we want to say. Whatever method works the best, guard your speech! Ensure that your marriage is not the victim of self-induced bitterness, pain, and distraction because of our words and/or how we say them.

Also, think about the example we set for others by how we talk to our spouses. Would you allow your kids to talk to you or your spouse like that? Would you want your kids to talk to their spouses like that? What about when your friends, coworkers, associates, and other people hear us speak to and about our spouses? Do we convey love and encouragement? Or are we essentially saying that our marriage is in trouble?

Those people may not be there when we apologize and make up. They may not see us make restitution with the person we've just crucified by our words and tone of voice. For all they know, based on what they heard us say, they may believe our marriage is headed for divorce. Actions speak louder than words, but our words reflect the action in our hearts. So we don't have a speech problem;

We don't have a speech problem; we have a heart problem.

we have a heart problem. Until we correct that, nothing will change. Your marriage matters, and so do your words.

 — *Taking a Minute for Your Marriage*

Consider the verse at the beginning of this chapter which teaches that our words originate from our hearts. Have you let comments leave your mouth that originated from a hurt deep in your heart? Give that pain to God at this moment so that He can perform miracles in how you talk to your spouse. Don't let the enemy use your words as tools of destruction; look for something kind and encouraging to speak to your spouse today!

CHAPTER 4

TIME

LIFE'S MOST PRECIOUS commodity is time. In a culture where people value homes, vehicles, athletic prowess, and education, among other things, we struggle to put a value on the most crucial thing—time. What we spend it on, we can't get back. We often fail to recognize the importance of time until we no longer have it. It truly does fly by.

Even in marriage, we can fail to maximize our time with our spouse and, in turn, *exist* instead of *thriving*. We can become roommates rather than soul mates. Quality time and quantity time both matter. So how do we make the most of it? How do we do as the Bible encourages us in Ephesians 5:16 when it says, "*make the best use of your time?*"

THE FOUR "RS" OF MARRIAGE

First off, we need to **REMEMBER the value of our time**. Vehicles lose value. Currency loses value. Clothes and other items lose their value and become obsolete. We've stated before how important marriage is to God and how important it should be to us. When something is of importance, it begins to gain value and worth in our eyes.

So if our marriage is designed to be of utmost importance, then it's safe to say the time we devote to building it and spending with our spouse should be just as important. That being said, how valuable is your marriage to you based on the time you give it? Would your spouse agree with your assessment?

Do you focus so much on advancing up the corporate ladder or making sure your kids are successful in their sports, school, and other endeavors that you neglect communicating and spending time with your spouse? Is the "guys' night out" or time with the girls more special to you than time with your spouse? Do you say "yes" to everyone and every opportunity that comes up and end up saying "no" to your spouse? If any of the above scenarios describe you, you may need to stop doing things that cause you to survive in marriage when you can have one that thrives.

Secondly, we must **REALIZE what we do with our time.** It's easy to quantify time as the number of hours spent doing something. For instance, businesses often pay based on hours per week worked. Our days are sectioned off into time frames that determine when we wake up, when we eat, when we work, what time we go to sleep, etc. Though these concepts show how we spend time and what we do with it, the thing that we fail to prioritize is what we do with our time when it comes to our marriage.

All the things mentioned above are good. They're essential. But if your marriage is lacking and struggling, it can severely affect all these areas. For example, if you and your spouse are arguing and at odds, it may cause your focus on your job to be skewed, which could impact your performance. Get in an argument with your spouse, and you could forsake eating. To give our spouses and marriages the value and worth they need, we must be determined and dedicated to protecting the time we have with them.

Doing things like eating together at home, carving out uninterrupted time for conversation, or spending moments together snuggling on the couch can make a huge difference. This may mean turning off your phone. The emails can wait. The texts don't have to be responded to immediately. Social media posting and scrolling can be put on hold. You can record the show for the sake of your marriage. You can create memories and happiness or bitterness and barriers.

Fight for time in your marriage. Make your marriage a top priority and let others know what you are doing so that they respect your decision not to take time away from your spouse to answer them, return that email, or go out that evening. If they disagree with your decision or give you a hard time, remember that you are married to your spouse, not them, and your spouse is your top priority.

Thirdly, we must **RECOGNIZE what time spent means.** Time spent can be summed up as a priority. What we prioritize, we make time for. For example, it's one thing to eat dinner together; it's another to be present at the meal both physically, emotionally, and mentally.

We must make sure that we are present while being present. People can tell when we're distracted or don't want to be

What we prioritize, we make time for.

somewhere. Does your spouse feel like they're unimportant to you because you're not all there? Do they get the leftovers while everyone and everything else gets your best? In this world, we will constantly be bombarded with issues, news, and notifications going off on our phones, demanding our time and focus. That's why we have to fight for our marriages.

We must wage war on these time attackers with unrivaled focus and precedence placed on our marriages. Is the time you spend on your marriage creating a meaningful relationship or one that is mundane? Is it based on priority or obligation? Would your spouse agree with your assessment?

When you near the end of your life, you're not going to reflect back and say, "I wish I had worked more hours, watched more shows, bought more things." But you might say you wish you would've invested more time in your marriage. So make your spouse a priority. Make the most of the time you have with them!

Lastly, we must **REFUSE to let anything steal time from our spouse.** In the hustle and bustle of life with jobs, kids, family and church obligations, and the myriad of other things we face daily, it's easy for something or someone to get put on the back burner. So often, we allow that to be our spouse and our marriage.

Countless marriages end due to irreconcilable differences. The argument could be made that the demands of everyday life erode our relationships ultimately to the point that many waste away to nothing. In these cases, that time with our spouse and the priority they should have is what gets removed.

We can become an island unto ourselves and watch marriages dissolve because our well-meaning intentions and the efforts we put in to balance all this stuff cause isolation. Again, the warning signs are evident: arguments, hostility, lack of communication, and many more.

Men, your wife craves stability. There's a great chance that stability in your marriage is more important to her than financial security. She wants to know that no matter what, you're with her forever. She may be stressed and overwhelmed with working, managing the home, and fulfilling her wifely role. And she needs to know you have her back!

Ladies, your husband needs to be respected and appreciated. Make a note of how hard he works. He needs to know that your kids aren't more important to you than he is. He would probably love to spend time with you just relaxing and doing nothing when he's off than have a litany of stuff to do on those days. Whatever the case, your spouse needs you to decide that, come what may, no *one* or no *thing* will replace you in value and importance.

Go on dates with your spouse! Let your kids see you make time for each other. Get away from the craziness and invest in each other. When you're on the date, be present! Talk, laugh, hold hands, kiss. Work on your relationship. Act as if there's nowhere else you would rather be and no one else you would rather be with.

The fact is that there are many couples who, if asked, would say they know that they need to make time for each other. But many of these couples never act on that. You can be different. Your marriage can be an example or a warning. In an age where time is of the essence, the essence of a successful marriage is passionately creating and protecting time with your spouse.

Please don't wait until it's your anniversary or another special occasion. Begin today. You and your spouse chose each other as lifelong marriage partners. Did you catch that? Each of you decided before God and others that this was the perfect person for you and your future.

This thought alone should stir within us an intense desire to give them the best of our energy and time. Don't compromise. Don't settle. Refuse to allow issues to fester and become a tragedy because everything seems okay.

God created you, your spouse, and your marriage for greatness. But for this to occur, significant effort must be made. So make them a priority by giving your time.

Be present.

Be available.

Be relentless.

Love can be spelled T-I-M-E. Don't make your spouse doubt your love by giving away your time. Instead, reassure them of your love by giving them your undivided, unrivaled time. You will be glad you did!

 — *Taking a Minute for Your Marriage*

We often don't realize that small things take a lot of time away from our relationships. One quick check of an email, one short phone call,

or a brief view of a social media post. Add these up, and you may have spent a considerable amount of time that could have been devoted to your loved ones. Assess how much attention you've given something or someone other than your spouse today. Then, determine to focus on changing these habits into something more productive.

CHAPTER 5

TREASURE

THE CONCEPT of treasure is very familiar in today's culture. Movies and books have been written about people making it their quest to find a hidden or buried treasure. It consumes them so that they spend their entire lives making it their mission to find it. Treasure can be defined as a "prized possession or entity." But, when it comes to the idea of marriage, is this a defining characteristic of your marriage? Do you cherish your marriage and spouse to the point of limiting your time in front of the TV for them? Is your marriage more precious than your golf game or hunting trip?

Scripture teaches that God considers us *the apple of His eye.* Because we are created in His image, we can have the ability to view things as He does. We have the capacity and capability to see our spouse as the apple of our eye. Sadly, as time goes by, our spouses can seem to become more of a burden than a gift. As money tightens, the kids come along, schedules become more chaotic, and our lives grow more challenging to manage. And we can be so caught up in the junk that we miss the precious treasure of our marriage.

Remember when you and your spouse were dating? If you weren't with them most of every day, chances are they were in your thoughts consistently. The way they wore their hair made you smile. The smell of their cologne or perfume was in your thoughts all day. They made your heart "pitter-patter."

However, the longer you are together, the easier it is to be "too comfortable" with each other. Once we get accustomed to our spouse, we take them for granted, and they no longer wow us like when we were dating.

The above instances exemplify how a marriage can go from being treasured and precious to losing its luster. The worth of something is synonymous with its value. Treasure is something that carries enormous worth or value. So let me ask this: How valuable is your marriage to you? Would your spouse agree with your assessment? Our spouses must feel valuable, or our marriages will crumble.

Maybe you grew up in a home where your worth depended on your performance. You were loved and accepted if you did well on a test, excelled athletically, didn't break the law, or kept from doing something to embarrass your parents. But should issues arise— you didn't make the honor roll, the Varsity team, or you simply forgot to take out the trash—suddenly, those you tried desperately to please turned away. They shunned or belittled you or even abused you in some tragic cases. If this describes your past, please know that your history doesn't have to determine your future. You can choose to change the cycle in your family, and that starts by treasuring your spouse.

To make our marriages precious and worthy of every bit of time, money, tears, and effort we put into them, we must start with a simple question. How do you see yourself and your spouse? Yes, neither one of you is perfect. But aside from that, what do you see?

Do you see a constant failure? Do you see someone ugly? Do you continuously compare yourself and your spouse with others and feel inferior or inadequate by doing so? If you can say "yes" to any of these questions, allow us to share a word of encouragement and hope.

Hebrews Chapter 6 teaches that it is impossible for God to lie. If He cannot lie, that means He is perfect. If He is perfect, then He does not make mistakes. Since God created everything—including you and your spouse—that means neither of you is a mistake. You were designed uniquely and specifically for a particular purpose. No one else in the world is exactly like the two of you! Since this is true, you must stop beating yourself and your spouse up. You were created in His image. He loves you so much that He was willing to die for you rather than live without you.

> *It is impossible for God to lie.*

It is so important when we run everything through this lens. You and your spouse's identities are not based on your limitations, faults, intelligence, metabolism, body shape, or other parameters the world places value on. Sure, your job is imperative. Certainly, having a roof over your head and food on the table is crucial. But these things do not define you.

You and your spouse are defined by a loving, perfect God that created you to know Him. He loves you just the way you are. He places immense value and worth on you and your spouse. You are so precious to Him that through Jesus Christ, He left the perfect place of Heaven to come live and deal with imperfect people. Then to prove His love further, He willingly died on the cross so those imperfect people could have eternal life.

Here's the deal: You and your spouse, though not perfect, are treasured by God. He can help you cherish each other. As His creation, looking at each other through His eyes will help you treasure one another.

FORGIVENESS AND UNDERSTANDING

Another way we can cultivate a precious and treasured marriage is by understanding and forgiving. Ladies, if you want your husband to be your "knight in shining armor" or the lead actor in your Hallmark movie, you must understand and forgive him. Understand the pressure he feels in today's culture. The demands to provide in a world of uncertainty are bombarding him. Yet, the desire to be a good husband and father is always at the center of his mind.

Men often won't tell you that for fear of looking weak. The best thing you can do is understand this, voice your support, and love and forgive him unconditionally. He is going to mess up. When he does, don't beat him up in your discussions. Are you giving your spouse a chance to share their side of the story, or are you adamant that you are always right and they need to come over to your side? Is your desire to be right blurring your vision of the situation? Clear and loving communication is the key to healing so that you can show your husband that you truly treasure him as the love of your life.

Guys, your wife needs you to understand and forgive her, as well. She needs you to understand why dinner may not be ready when you get home. She needs you to be okay if the house isn't immaculate all the time. Your wife needs you to forgive and understand when she is too tired to be intimate. She, too, has demands placed on her. In addition to being there for you, she may have to fulfill the role of mother, employer, team mom, chauffeur, and so on.

She often feels overwhelmed by the insurmountable list of things on her plate. Forgive her if the laundry piles up. Understand what her day has been like when you come in from work, and she is at her "wit's end."

For us to forgive and understand, we must communicate. There needs to be freedom to openly and honestly share our feelings without fear or worry that what we say will escalate into an argument. Your spouse doesn't know how you feel in many cases.

They can't read your mind. So cut them some slack and share your feelings.

Start affirming them by telling them how much you want your marriage to thrive. Proceed then into telling them what's bothering you. Help them understand, and then forgive them for not understanding you. Forgive them, and then move on. Don't keep bringing it up or holding things against your spouse.

Forgiveness and understanding are vital to the health of your marriage. And truth be told, if you value your spouse, you should be willing to forgive, understand and sacrifice for them.

Maybe that means you sacrifice being right.

Maybe you sacrifice a trip or outing to help alleviate the stress your spouse has incurred.

Maybe you need to forgive them for being focused on the demands of life they're dealing with that they didn't consider all you do. Understand how they feel. Understand you're in this together.

So to put this in a nutshell, you and your spouse can have a marriage that is a treasure, not a burden. It will take work. It will be hard. But it will be rewarding. It will be worth it. You and your spouse are not perfect but are created by a perfect God who knows what He's doing. Forgive and understand each other. Don't let your identity be wrapped up in peripheral things that don't matter. Find your identity and worth in Jesus. Let Him and His love encourage you. Do this, and your marriage will be the treasure God designed it to be! It will be worth it!

⏳ — *Taking a Minute for Your Marriage*

Forgiveness is often confused with forget-ness. It can be difficult to forget a hurt or adverse event that sticks in our memory. And that makes it harder to forgive. Have a conversation with your spouse about what forgiveness means to each of you. Be respectful of their viewpoint. Listen, ask questions, and gain insight. Remind yourselves that we can forgive each other because Christ has forgiven us.

CHAPTER 6

TEACHING

HAVE YOU EVER THOUGHT of your marriage as an opportunity to teach? Believe it or not, we teach our spouses, kids, family, friends, and even strangers a lot about marriage through how we interact with our spouses. But, in reality, we teach, in most cases, what we have learned or been taught. Therefore, it's safe to say that what our marriages teach others is directly correlated to what we observed or were taught about marriage by others. As long as we live, we are still learning and being taught. So, the question is, what are we teaching? Are we proud or ashamed of what we teach others through our marriage?

Now that we have laid the groundwork for the idea of our marriages being an outlet for teaching, let's examine *what* is being taught and if we are okay with it. We will review a couple of the many things taught in marriage, starting with one of the most widely used but least understood words in the human language. It's a word we throw around flippantly like we would dirty clothes or trash.

The term is LOVE, and if you stop and think about it, you'd probably agree that the word is commonly misunderstood in today's culture. We glibly say we "love" this or "love" that when referring to people and things that mean very little in the grand scheme of things. And our spouses don't need to be grouped with these numerous other things which vie for our affection. Instead, our love for them should be so vibrant and ever-growing that all these other loves should be moved to the "friend zone," not the other way around.

In Ephesians 5, the Bible says that husbands should love their wives as Christ loved the church and gave himself up for her. That means that showing you love her won't always be easy. There will be times, such as following an argument, when sacrificing for her won't be at the forefront of our minds. That's why love must be unconditional. For us to love this way, we must experience the love of God. We love because He first loved us. So, are you teaching others to love their spouses unconditionally, when it's convenient, or on special occasions?

Likewise, ladies, you can demonstrate love for your husband by listening to him without trying to fix him. There will be times when he makes a mistake, and this is where you model that unconditional love. You don't always have to rush in and fix every problem; sometimes, he just needs you to be there for him. During this time, encourage and honor him, but don't belittle or berate him.

We teach people about conflict resolution through how we deal with it in marriage.

We can also teach people about conflict resolution through how we deal with it in marriage. Conflict is inevitable. It's going to happen. But one of the main problems in marriage is allowing unresolved conflict to fester into a huge problem that can ultimately lead to pain, heartache, betrayal, and divorce. We believe there are numerous ways to handle conflict; we will discuss three.

THREE WAYS TO HANDLE CONFLICT PRODUCTIVELY

First is **how we FIGHT.** Fighting is the typical course of action for many couples. They get into a disagreement beset by emotion and pride that spills over into an argument that can involve yelling, hurtful comments, and, sadly, violence. Most people don't know how to fight fair. Like the kids in the schoolyard duking it out, we emotionally lash out and do whatever we can to hurt our opponent. Fight fair. Let each other share their feelings and thoughts without thinking of a comeback and waiting for your chance to pounce verbally. Truly listen with the intent of restoration, not condemnation.

The second area of conflict resolution is **taking FLIGHT,** or what is commonly known as the avoidance principle. It involves one or both parties leaving and fleeing to avoid further damage. In most cases, flight leads to pent-up hostility and anger because we don't honestly share our feelings and get everything out in the open. We bottle it up. We become distant. Maybe we disconnect emotionally. Perhaps we leave permanently. Either way, the goal is to punish our spouses by withholding from them.

Then the breaking point comes, and the volcano erupts. The bottom falls out. If this is you, understand that sometimes it's okay to walk away and gather your thoughts. It's OK to use this time to regain your composure.

But it can't be an all-the-time thing. In our opinion, the more you flee without working out your differences, the easier it gets to flee—maybe not physically from your house but emotionally, spiritually, and from the role you are called to fill in your marriage.

And that brings us to the third way to handle and manage conflict: **make RIGHT.** Jesus had people mad at Him many times. It's evident that He dealt with conflict just as we do, but His desire was for us to make things right and restore the relationship. Look at what He says. "So if you are offering your gift at the altar and there remember that your brother has something against you, leave your gift there before the altar and go. First, be reconciled to your brother, and then come and offer your gift." (Matthew 5:23-24 ESV)

This belief is contrary to everything we have been taught. We are instructed to get revenge or to make it bad for whomever we're in conflict with—no matter the cost. Jesus flips this thinking around and challenges us to look past our pride and grudges and make things right. Apologize, offer forgiveness, and don't withhold it.

Remember why you married your spouse. Understand that neither of you is perfect, and you make mistakes, too. Reconciliation is crucial to marriage. Joy and happiness in marriage are available and can be experienced. Reconciliation is the key.

The Apostle Paul shared a similar thought when he shared:

Be angry and do not sin; do not let the sun go down on your anger.
EPHESIANS 4:26 ESV

When he was known as Saul, Paul was the epitome of conflict. He persecuted and killed Christians. He was part of the crowd that would stir up conflict in towns because he didn't like what was happening. After encountering Christ, he becomes Paul and pens the above passage.

Paul encourages us to go to great lengths to make things right. The outcome is never good when we allow anger to rule our lives. We lash out—we say things we don't mean. We inflict pain. So what do we do? Work out the situation. Even if you stay up all night, make it right. Talk it out. Write a letter to your spouse. Calmly discuss issues. Pray together. Refuse to let Satan have a foothold in your marriage caused by anger.

Misery loves company. That's why we continually have problems when we talk to people at the office or a trusted friend about our marriage instead of talking to God and each other about it. Most of the time, those well-meaning people may give you worldly and emotionally-driven advice rather than godly advice that is restoration driven. The result is terrible. Anger breeds resentment—love breeds restoration.

Remember, we are teaching others through our marriages. So what are you teaching concerning love and conflict resolution? Would your spouse agree? What can you do to change this for the better, making your marriage one that teaches that love and conflict resolution resulting in better marriage and not a bitter one?

— *Taking a Minute for Your Marriage*

You may have heard the modern-day proverb, "More is caught than taught." A paraphrase of this proverb is, "Actions speak louder than words." Regardless of how you phrase it, this is an essential piece of advice when it comes to what you are teaching others through the actions of your marriage. Consider for a moment the wrong lessons others may have caught from your poor actions toward your spouse. Are you willing to change for the better to be a better testimony of true love in your relationship?

CHAPTER 7

TRAPS

JUST LIKE IN HUNTING or rodent removal, where traps are set to catch prey, Satan, our enemy, sets traps for us. His plan with these traps is to kill, steal, and destroy. He wants to kill your dream of a great marriage. He desires to steal the joy in your marriage and ultimately sets out to destroy our marriages and lives. His traps, like others we set, are clever in their design and enticing with their lure of what we perceive to be harmless beauty.

This beauty, though, is far from harmless. Once engulfed in the trap, we quickly discover that what once seemed beautiful has turned into a destructive, nasty, devastating poison that kills. These traps are everywhere; sadly, many marriages and lives succumb to the chaos they cause. They are wrapped up into three main categories.

In fact, Jesus Himself was faced with these same traps, but unlike us, He didn't give in to them. Because He didn't get trapped, we can turn to Him as the answer and as the person to look to help us avoid them altogether. So what are these categories where Satan places these traps? Let's look at them together.

THE MAJOR TRAPS OF THE ENEMY

The first category of traps is **LUST OF THE FLESH.** Before Jesus began His ministry, He embarked on a 40-day fast. During this time in the desert, He was tempted by Satan. Since the devil is crafty and cunning in nature, he comes to attack Jesus when He is weak. The first attack is with food. Satan tries to trap Him by saying that if Jesus was really God, He should prove it by turning stones into bread. Bread was a staple in that culture. It was a part of every meal in ancient Jewish times. Satan knew Jesus was hungry, and he attacked with that enticing trap.

But Jesus didn't buckle. He didn't give in. We don't have to either. Unfortunately, many of us fall into this trap and use our weaknesses as an excuse.

Maybe you come in from work exhausted and want some downtime. To decompress, you grab a device, surf the net, and inadvertently images cross the screen that begin to engross you. The trap now has you; before you know it, you're spending more time and maybe even money satisfying the raging fire that consumes you and less time with your spouse and kids.

You try your best to hide your addiction, but it comes out. Your marriage is in peril. Your spouse is devastated. Your marriage is wrecked, and you may even lose your kids and/or job. The people you've been looking at don't care about what happened to you. Your momentary excitement made them tons of money and cost you everything. The trap gets another one.

The second category where traps linger is **LUST OF THE EYES.** After Satan failed to get Jesus to bite the first time, He tried again. This time Satan appeals to Jesus' human nature of acting on what's attractive to us. You know, the "eye candy." Whether it's a person, a thing we can't live without, the latest and greatest gadget, or anything else that catches our eye, we all struggle with it.

Our world is full of advertisements, entertainment, and images that bombard our eyes and, ultimately, our minds with the idea that we have to get what we see. Satan tells Jesus that if He threw Himself down from the pinnacle of the temple, God would send his angels down to save Him, which would circumvent the plan God had to save humanity from their sins through the death of Jesus. It was an easy way out for Him. The opportunity to take what appeared better for what was ultimately the best.

Because we are so concerned with others' approval and how we look in their eyes, we do the same thing. Our image is sacrificed at the altar of status and fame. In marriage, we pay to the hilt for things we can't afford. We try to create an image of marriage that portrays perfection and idyllic perception. Even social media accounts reek of pictures and images that cater to the craving to be someone and look good to others.

The third category is **PRIDE OF LIFE.** Satan's third trap for Jesus (*and for us*) is entirely based on this. He told Jesus that if He bowed in worship, all the world's kingdoms would be given to Him. But the issue is that it wasn't Satan's to give. Jesus, as God in the flesh, is Lord over *everything*.

Essentially, Satan bombards us with the idea that everything is about us and what we want. Pride is about self. It's about us getting what we want. In marriage, this trap comes when we would rather be right than be united. We want what we want when we want it. Many marriages disintegrate because of pride. One spouse gets mad because they don't get what they want. Therefore, they seek what they want elsewhere. Pride leads to isolation, frustration, and hostility.

Marriage must be characterized by two partners giving 100 percent daily to the other person. Jesus modeled selflessness and humility perfectly. Scripture says that though He was God, He didn't use that as a means to get followers; instead, we are told He humbled Himself and served. He realized the greatest way to attract people to Him was by loving and serving them.

> *Marriage must be characterized by two partners giving 100% every day to the other person.*

Pride repels. Humility and service attract. Are you so proud that it's your way or the highway? Does your spouse feel like they can do nothing right? Are you more concerned about being right and your agenda being followed than seeing your marriage be whole and thrive? If so, Satan has trapped you with this.

Maybe your marriage doesn't struggle with these traps right now. Great! Just be prepared because Satan will still come after you at some point. He tends to pounce when we're tired, weak, and emotionally or spiritually spent. So be ready.

Draw near to Jesus and your spouse. Ask for forgiveness. Serve one another. Say no to the eye candy. I Corinthians 10:13 teaches that when temptation comes, God always provides a way of escape. He always supplies an out. Look for that escape hatch. Don't flirt with sin. Flee from it. Don't give Satan an inch, or he will take a mile!

 — *Taking a Minute for Your Marriage*

This chapter discusses three primary traps that our enemy, Satan, uses to catch or trip us up: Lust of the flesh, the lust of the eyes, and pride of life. Which of these presents itself most often within your relationship? Are you feeling ensnared by one or more of these currently? Then ask the Lord to provide a way out—an escape—so that you may be free to walk in the covenant marriage God has for you.

SECTION 2

WHAT'S IN YOUR MARRIAGE TOOLBELT?

CHAPTER 8

MARRIAGE TOOLBELT TOOL #1 - CHOOSE

AUTHOR'S NOTE: Building something well requires the correct tools. Marriage is no different—it requires specific skills and actions to build a relationship that will withstand the trials of time. This next section will discuss critical tools to carry within your proverbial toolbelt to construct a solid and healthy marriage.

THE FIRST TOOL that needs to be in our marriage toolbelt is one we must constantly use because areas of our marriage must be worked on and tinkered with daily. Time has to be allocated. Sacrifices must be prevalent. And ultimately, a decision, a choice, must be made. Every day we must **CHOOSE** to be married. We must choose to work on marriage and fight for it.

But like other projects, if we don't use this tool, the issues and problems that occur will lead to more significant issues and ultimately cause us to quit or give up. Like many unfinished projects we've given up on, marriages are dissolved because things get complicated, and we get frustrated.

In Joshua 24:15, Joshua, the great leader of the nation of Israel, is nearing the end of his life. He draws a line in the sand and makes a definitive statement. He lays everything on the line and says,

"Choose TODAY (*emphasis added*) whom you will serve, as for me and my house we *will* serve the Lord." Joshua tells his people that no matter what they do or think about what he does, he has made his choice: He will follow God at all costs. Joshua went all chips in. Just like he chose, we must choose. And we must choose daily.

When you became married, you made a choice. And if you remember, especially if you recited the traditional vows, you committed to making the choice "until death, do you part." The problem is that many times we say these words, but we don't truly mean them from our hearts. The world is filled with couples who one day stood before a group of people and God, stating that they chose one another. But it was only based on emotion and not on a commitment willing to weather hard times and struggles that come with marriage.

We say I'll choose to be married as long as I'm happy. I'll choose to be married until a better proposition comes along. My husband doesn't get me, so it's okay to leave him. My wife neglects me, so I choose to end my marriage.

That's why every day you have to choose.

Understand that you will have hard days and challenging times in marriage. That's why every day you have to choose. You must choose to love, forgive, and stay despite what everyone else says, thinks, or does. So, remaining married and thriving in marriage is a *daily* choosing. But it's also something else.

Staying married and thriving is also a **DEDICATED CHOOSING.** Notice that Joshua says he and his family *will* serve the Lord. Your marriage can survive. It can last. It can prosper and thrive. But marriage is not about cans; it's about wills. Will yours?

When it comes to the idea of will, it comes down to dedication. Saying "I will" articulates that the line has been drawn. There's no turning back. I chose you for marriage, and I choose you today and forever.

When you don't like your spouse, will you still choose them? Will you still choose them when finances are low and stress is high? When they let you down, will you still choose to say "yes?" You certainly can. But *will* you?

Will you choose them today? Will you be dedicated to them today? We choose to do many things. We choose to accept the job. We choose where and what we eat. We choose where to go and what to do on vacation. Life is full of choices. But the question is: Will you choose your spouse? Will you choose them daily? Will you choose them in dedication?

Finally, choosing your spouse is a **DIFFERENT CHOOSING.** Before Joshua made his definitive statement, he said, "If it is unacceptable in your eyes to serve the Lord, choose today whom you will serve: the gods your fathers served...or the one true God."

Did you catch it? Joshua knew the trend. He knew well how culture, society, and popular opinion influenced the Israelites and their decision to follow God. He understood that choosing to follow God would alienate him. It would cause him to look foolish in others' eyes, yet he was willing to put all that aside in devotion and genuine commitment. He was willing to be different than everyone else. Are you?

Epidemics of divorce, separation, and living together without being married are at an all-time high. It's almost become socially acceptable to leave when things get tough. The old adage "everyone's doing it" seems to apply to these harsh realities more than ever before.

The truth is: Not *everyone* is doing it, and you don't have to either. You can be different. You can choose to weather the storms that will come and stay together. Will you choose? Will you fight? The choice is yours.

— Taking a Minute for Your Marriage

You've probably heard the phrase, "When the going gets tough, the tough get going." Marriage is hard work. And there are times when it is easier to simply remove ourselves from difficult situations. You may think, "I'm going to get going. I want out."

But God's ways are always higher. He says, "Choose to remain in [fill in the blank], and I will be with you." So ask God today to give you wisdom on choosing His way over the world's way. Make a firm decision to put Him first and seek His help in becoming dedicated to your spouse and marriage.

CHAPTER 9

MARRIAGE TOOLBELT TOOL #2 - CELEBRATE

IN OUR CULTURE, we celebrate numerous events from the very beginning of life, including gender reveals, a baby's first steps, and first birthdays. We post celebrations on social media, such as little league wins and recital performances. Accolades, awards, special occasions, and even celebrities garner celebration.

A couple of things that tend to be less celebrated and applauded are marriage and spouses. Except for birthdays, anniversaries, and other notable dates and achievements, we often let the adulation and celebration of these things wane. Maybe it's because we get used to one another over time. Perhaps it's because we think our spouse knows how we feel, so they don't need to be applauded.

But amidst all of the chaos and craziness in the world, if there's anything that needs to be celebrated and honored, it is these two vital things—our spouse and our marriage. After all, since marriage is the first institution created between a man and woman, it should be the most celebrated earthly entity in our lives.

Maybe you are single and desire to be married one day. Then, celebrate marriage, and don't settle for anyone other than the one God created perfectly for you.

The Bible takes a celebratory view of marriage. For example, in the book of Proverbs, King Solomon, the wisest and richest man on the planet at the time, encourages us with these words:

> *Rejoice in the wife of your youth. Be intoxicated always in her love.*
> PROVERBS 5:18-19

These words convey celebration in a big way. Solomon says, "Rejoice and be intoxicated always in your relationship."

- When was the last time you were ecstatic about your marriage?
- When was the last time you viewed it with joy and not dread?
- How different would our marriages be if we looked at them this way?

In our world, we can get intoxicated or drunk on many things. Why not your spouse? Whereas intoxication from alcohol, greed, power, or even Krispy Kreme doughnuts can bring us misery and regret, doesn't it make sense that being captivated by our spouses in this way would bring us joy and excitement? If these other things can hurt, surely the love of and for our spouses should cause us to give them more attention and celebration.

Men, your wife needs to hear you speak highly of her. She wants her kids and others to know that she still captivates you even as she ages. When clothes don't fit her like they once did, or when her hair turns from the color it was when you first saw her, she still needs you to let her and others know she's more beautiful than ever. She must be celebrated for what she does and who she is, both in and outside your home.

Hold her hand. Put your arm around her in public.

You can be assured that celebrating her will not go unnoticed, and you will be glad it doesn't. Hold her hand. Put your arm around her in public. Celebrate her in front of others.

Ladies, if you want your husband to continue to be your knight in shining armor, celebrate him. Stop nagging and start celebrating. Edify him to other wives. Praise him in front of your friends and family. Post about him on social media. Let him know that though he may have more hair in his ears and nose than on his head, he is still attractive to you. He may have more of a "dad bod" than a Hollywood movie star body, but he needs you to let him know that his body is the one you want. When you do, he'll become ten feet tall and bulletproof.

Best-selling author Emerson Eggerich writes that respect is a man's #1 need. So, celebrate him by respecting him. Value his opinion; don't emasculate him by acting as if his views and decisions don't matter. Be on his side. Don't side with others over him.

Guys, this goes for you too! Your kids, parents, and friends are not who you married. Therefore, their opinions and schedules should not be your first priority. Valuing your spouse's opinions above others will help her to know that she is celebrated by you.

Singles—celebrate being single. God has someone for you. Perhaps He's waiting to provide you that special someone until you're both ready. He is working to handcraft you and make you into the woman or man he wants you to be. Don't rush it. He has a plan! Stop settling for spam when He's got a prime rib waiting for you! When the day comes to get married, you will be fully prepared for the one who has been fully prepared for you.

Adam waited to be given his wife, Eve. You can wait too. Celebrate now so you can celebrate each other in the future.

 — Taking a Minute for Your Marriage

At the root of any celebration is the acknowledgment of something important or done well. For example, we celebrate a promotion at work, an "A" on a test, or the completion of a course of study.

What has your spouse done or accomplished that you can celebrate on this day? Praise them for the big and small things that bring joy and excitement to your relationship. Perhaps surprise them with a simple gesture of love and admiration. Pay them a compliment or send them an encouraging text to celebrate them.

CHAPTER 10

MARRIAGE TOOLBELT TOOL #3 – COUNTERCULTURE MARRIAGE

WE ARE VERY MUCH people that imitate others. We wear what's in style because we see others wearing it and want to be trendy. We dance around like fools because we are trying out the latest TikTok moves. We rush to the movie theater to see that new movie because everyone is talking about it on Facebook. Common lingo and words are copied and used for relevance depending on the generation. The bottom line is we imitate and copy what seems to be societal trends.

Sadly, another thing that seems to be copied is ending a marriage. All across the globe, divorce is running rampant. We probably all know someone that's experienced divorce, or we may have gone through it ourselves. If marriage is the most vital human relationship we have, why are so many ending it before death do them part?

The answer is pretty simple, we imitate others. Unfortunately, statistics say you might be inclined to divorce if you were raised in a broken home. This cycle of behavior can be broken in your family by the power of God. Still, it would be best to analyze whether your actions represent the belief system you developed as a child. Also, suppose most of your time is spent around single people bragging about how happy they are that they escaped from their marriage. In that case, you are likely to begin to believe what they are saying and wish you were single too. Consequently, it is just in our nature to want to fit in, and to do that we often imitate the actions of others.

The Bible speaks to this issue. According to the following passage, the problem existed in those times as well:

Do not be conformed any longer to the patterns (customs) of the world. But be transformed by the renewing of your mind.
ROMANS 12:2 NIV

There are two parts to this verse that will help us understand that not everything in the world should be copied: Refusal and Renewal. We will discuss each one and see how they apply.

The first is **REFUSAL.** Paul says, "Do not conform." That implies a decision or a firm commitment that says, "Ending our marriage in divorce is not an option!" In fact, you must refuse to even let it be part of the conversation when things are difficult and not going according to your liking.

Our marriage is based on this. We both came from different home situations. Teresa is a product of divorce and lived with the constant flip-flopping between her parents while growing up. Jon had parents that were married for over 40 years. Even though the results of our parents' marriages were drastically different, we both refused to let divorce be an option. Even in disagreements, we do not mention the "D" word. Simply put: We refuse to!

We will not be another statistic. We refuse to let the common trend of divorce and what others do in their marriage be like that in ours. Instead, we choose to work out our issues and problems and stay together rather than let those things divide us and split us up. There is strength in numbers, and two of us together are far better than one of us going it alone.

The second thing Paul says we can use to prevent divorce and heartache is **RENEWAL.** He states that we can be transformed. Or, as the Amplified Bible says, "We can be progressively changed by renewing our minds." To do this, we have to exchange commonly held ideas and theories that promote taking the path of least resistance and giving up on each other for the concept of staying together and changing to be better.

Imagine what would happen if we stayed and worked things out instead of bolting. If our commitment to our marriage was so strong that we were willing to do whatever it took to restore it. What if we asked God to change *us* before we asked Him to get ahold of our spouse? What if we recognized that God has the power to transform and renew anything that is broken.

The Greek words for "transformed" and "renewing" can be translated as "metamorphosis" and "renovation." This conveys that God can take our battered and broken marriages and do a complete turnaround where beauty can be seen, and healing is evident. Like a house that gets remade from a dilapidated eye sore to a stunning HGTV dream home, our marriages can come from the brink of despair and destruction to one of picture-perfect health. But it starts with how we think about marriage and divorce. When we change our minds and start thinking about remodeling our marriage, tearing it down with a divorce won't be an option.

What we put in our minds comes out in our lives and actions. Therefore, if we are constantly bombarding our senses and thoughts with the grass is greener, and I would be happy if I weren't with them, then we will find it easier to say "yes" to divorce and "no" to marriage.

What we put in our minds comes out in our lives and actions.

Conversely, if we allow God's Word to penetrate our minds with His idea on marriage and hang around with people who have been and are committed to being married for life, we will be far more inclined to stay together. Misery loves company. Birds of a feather flock together. These well-known phrases are absolutely accurate. Maybe the thing that is keeping your marriage from flourishing and surviving is the people you're associated with. Refuse to be like the world. Renew your mind. Be counter-cultural in your marriage. Stand out; don't fit in!

 — Taking a Minute for Your Marriage

Often, we don't realize the powerful influence people have on our lives. The world seeks to mold us, and we may not feel the squeeze until it's too late.

Are there people in your life who exercise too much influence over you or over your marriage? Do we follow their views and make decisions based on their perspective rather than God's? Ask the Holy Spirit to show you areas where imitating someone else is not healthy for your marriage. Choose to walk in a way that doesn't conform to the world's standards. Renew your mind this day.

CHAPTER 11

MARRIAGE TOOLBELT TOOL #4 – CULTIVATE

HAVE YOU EVER LOOKED at a basket full of vibrant, ripe vegetables or a tree bursting forth with fresh fruit? Neither the vegetables nor the fruit just happened to sprout up. It wasn't by chance that they ripened and grew. It took work and cultivation to bring about the results that the gardener, planter of the tree, or farmer desired. We, as consumers, are the beneficiaries of the ripeness and freshness of the product resulting from that hard work.

The same is true with growing our marriage. For us to get the desired results, it takes hard work. A good marriage requires cultivation. Cultivating a marriage involves a few key aspects.

The first aspect is **KNOWING.** The gardener and farmer must know the conditions, the seed, and the care needed to produce the desired crop. They diligently add water, soil, sunlight, and other beneficial things to what's planted to facilitate growth. The more time they spend on the crops, the more they know what works and what doesn't.

Apply this to your marriage. How well do you know your spouse? Do you know what works and what doesn't? It's easy to say "yes," but as crops grow and evolve over time, so do marriages.

We can't assume that what worked last year, last month, last week, or even yesterday will work today. Your spouse will change. Their opinions, likes, and dislikes may change. And, if we don't spend time getting to know them, we can miss out on a marriage that ripens to full maturity and instead end up with one that rots and sours.

This knowledge is more than head knowledge. We can know a ton of information about our spouses. But if we're not getting to know them from the heart intimately, we won't produce what we want from our marriages.

Matthew 15:8 speaks to this concept of head knowledge. Jesus confronts religious leaders who studied and understood the religious law so well that they would quote it and condemn anyone they felt went against what they knew. They puffed themselves up about their knowledge and considered themselves better than everyone else. Our marriages can become like this when we think we've got it all figured out and assume we know how our spouse feels or what they want. Instead, we must take time to connect with them and understand them from the heart.

The second aspect of cultivation is **GROWING**. Those that tend crops aren't satisfied with a bit of growth. They don't just drop the seed in the ground and expect that seed to produce tasty treats. They focus on growing the crop. Leadership expert John Addison says that we're either ripening or rotting. The determining factor between these two is growth and our emphasis on it.

Marriages stop growing because spouses stop growing.

As times change, we must change. We should desire to be better today than we were yesterday and better tomorrow than we were today. Marriages stop growing because spouses stop growing. In many cases, we get set in our ways and become content with status-quo relationships that produce boredom and frustration.

Try something new. Read books. Listen to a marriage podcast. Get involved in a Bible-proclaiming church and attend small group studies with other married couples. Seek mentorship with others who have been married longer than you. Go to a marriage enrichment event. Don't ask and expect your spouse to change and grow if you're unwilling to yourself.

Several times in Scripture, writers use the idea of milk and solid food to reinforce this idea. When milk is mentioned in this context, it's talking about those who should be more mature and fully grown or growing in spiritual matters. The same holds true in marriage. Many couples should be farther ahead than they are. Their marriage should not be struggling with the same things it did when it was new. In essence, many couples, no matter how long they've been married, are babies in their growth when they should be fully grown. The end result is a disaster! It's like a toddler trying to handle adult problems and issues, which doesn't work out so well.

The third and final aspect of cultivation is **SHOWING.** As we seek to know our spouses better and grow as people, we will begin to show the fruit of a healthy marriage. We begin to be an example to others of what marriage can and should be. If we want our marriages to be examples and not warnings, we need to know our spouses and grow to be the person they desire and deserve, so we can show anyone who sees us that marriage is beautiful and worth fighting for.

⧗ — *Taking a Minute for Your Marriage*

When a couple first begins dating, they talk for hours, excited to learn everything they can about each other. But much of that goes away as the years move on. Studies show that many couples talk for less than thirty minutes a day. Some couples say they briefly chat during meals, while others say they do so before going to sleep.

What time investment are you currently putting into focused dialogue with your spouse? Do you carve time out of the day to converse and learn more about each other? Before heading off to bed, ensure that you prioritize having a healthy conversation. Making this a priority will help produce a fruitful marriage.

SECTION 3

PUTTING THE QUALI-"T" BACK INTO YOUR MARRIAGE

CHAPTER 12

THANKFULNESS

OIL AND WATER. Zits and prom night. Pizza Buffets and low-carb diets. These are all things that obviously don't go well together. In fact, mix any of these and their respective partner together, and agony will ensue.

The same incompatibility could be seen when it comes to a complaining spirit and thankfulness. In fact, it's almost impossible for a complaining attitude and a thankful heart to coexist. Try it. See if you can be bitter while giving thanks. Do an experiment and see if the number of complaints you have come close to equaling what you have to be thankful for.

When it comes to thankfulness and complaining, which would you say characterizes your marriage more? And when we stop and consider how much we have to be thankful for, as it pertains to marriage, why would we choose anything else but that? So let's look at some things we must be grateful for in marriage.

The first is **PARTNERSHIP**. In Genesis 2:18, God, who created marriage, states that "it's not good for man to be alone." He understood and created us with a need for partnership and relationship. The passage of Scripture goes on to say that God would give the man a helper suitable for him. How cool is this?

We can be thankful that God has already given us a person perfectly suitable for us. If you're not married, just know that you can be thankful that God has someone for you, and you can trust in His timing and plan to bring that person to you. We should be thankful that He loves us enough to provide a person that will balance us and complete us for life. Instead of complaining about your spouse, be appreciative that you have one and don't have to go it alone. If you've lost your spouse, be thankful for the time and lessons God gave you with them and trust that He is working for you to help you deal with that loss.

God has already given us a person made perfectly suitable for us.

The second thing we should be thankful for in marriage is **PLEASURE**. The same God that created marriage between a man and woman also created sex and the pleasure that comes with it. When sex is in the confines of a marriage relationship between a man and a woman, the way God intends it, the pleasure that is generated is unimaginable because it's perfect.

It's not just momentary and fleeting. It's not dirty or shameful. It's beautiful and makes the marriage covenant special. When people seek sexual gratification outside of marriage with someone else, through pornography or other ways, pleasure is replaced with lust and, ultimately, addiction and destruction. That's why affairs, pornographic addictions, and other cheap thrills—though visibly enticing and alluring—cause so much pain.

Simply put, pleasure in sex that is long-lasting and meaningful is only available in a marriage union between husband and wife. We should be thankful that God cares about us so much that he created sex and created it to be pleasurable, powerful, and meaningful. When we understand that this is reserved only for our spouse, it adds to the pleasure.

Wives—stop complaining about your husband's sex drive and need for it all the time. Instead, be thankful that he desires you.

Likewise, men, stop complaining that your wife doesn't give it to you enough. Instead, be grateful that when it does happen, it will be incredibly pleasurable the way God orchestrated it.

The third reason we have to be thankful in marriage is the **PICTURE** it gives. There may not be a more adequate picture of God's unconditional love and forgiveness, made known through the death and resurrection of Jesus Christ, than in a marriage. In the same way, we choose to forgive our mate's faults and errors and still love them, Jesus chose to forgive us for every mess-up we would ever commit. He showed us how much he loved and forgave us by willingly and sacrificially giving His life on the cross for us.

> *But God shows his love for us in that while we were*
> *still sinners, Christ died for us.*
> ROMANS 5:8 ESV

We can be thankful that God desires to use our marriages as a living picture of what He did for us. By choosing to love and forgive each other, even when they don't deserve it, we can point people to the God that loves and forgives them. When we love our spouses unconditionally and don't make them feel like they have to earn our love, we paint a picture of God's love for us.

So instead of complaining about all your spouse's wrongdoings, be thankful that God chose you to model forgiveness and love that can point others to Him. Stop complaining and start thanking!

⏳ — *Taking a Minute for Your Marriage*

The Bible says that two are better than one, as it speaks to the unity that comes with marriage. Therefore, God created us to be suitable complements to our spouses. The word complement comes from the

Latin complére, meaning "to complete." So, in marriage, neither a man nor a woman is whole without the other.

But Satan would have us overfocus on our differences rather than view them as something that helps to fulfill or unify us. What strengths and talents in your spouse complement your gifts and graces? Begin to see those differences as God's gift to complete you.

CHAPTER 13

TEMPERATURE OF MARRIAGE

TEMPERATURE IS A crucial thing to know. It determines what we wear and whether we stay inside or outside. Temperature can cause atmospheric conditions that can affect our day-to-day lives. For instance, schools and businesses can close if the temperature dips below freezing and is accompanied by freezing rain, ice, snow, and slick roads. We have probably seen or been made aware of fires throughout our nation due to consistently dry days without rain. Mix those arid conditions with temperatures over 100 degrees; the effects are sometimes catastrophic.

Have you ever thought about temperature as it pertains to your marriage? More than likely, you haven't, and admittedly, up until this writing, we hadn't either! So let's delve deeper into the subject using three different temperature settings: hot, cold, and lukewarm. Everyone has likely experienced water or food at one of these levels. Each of these can have positive or negative consequences on us. These three levels are even outlined and discussed in Revelation 3.

In verse 15 of Revelation, Chapter 3, John speaks a message to a church that comes directly from Jesus. Since Jesus refers to *us* as His bride, we can apply this to our marriage.

The church Jesus is speaking to here is the Church of Laodicea. The church did not have a natural water source in the town of Laodicea, and they were forced to use aqueducts to bring water from neighboring towns. One neighboring town had cold springs, and another had hot springs, both refreshing in their own ways. However, when the water was pumped to Laodicea, it was neither hot nor cold—just lukewarm.

The first temperature of marriage is **COLD.** Have you ever come in from outside after the sun had beaten hard down upon you? Once you got inside, wasn't it refreshing to have the air conditioner and an ice-cold glass of water available? Our marriages should be like this for our spouses and for others.

When we are around each other, we should be infused with life and have our days refreshed. You and your spouse should refresh and invigorate each other instead of nagging and depleting the other. How we love and enjoy our spouse should also be a refreshing sign to those who aren't married or struggling in their marriage. Is your marriage that way? Jesus said in this passage that He wishes we were cold or hot, which brings us to the second temperature.

Is your marriage **HOT?** No, not that romantically charged hotness that everyone associates with the word. Though important, that's not the angle we are approaching here. When Jesus told John that he wished that the church was "hot," he said it in the sense of healing and therapeutic.

Ever taken a nice hot bath or shower? Remember how healing and therapeutic it felt on your sore and weary body? Jesus wanted this church to be where people could find healing and help. Your marriage is no different. Your spouse should be able to look to you for help. They should never feel like we are too distant or busy to help them.

Guys, take your wife's call. The meeting and business can wait. Ladies, respond to his text or call when he's at the grocery store.

The conversation with your girlfriend, your favorite show, or even the laundry or dishes can wait till you give him the help he needs. Other people need to see your marriage as a place where they can find help and maybe even healing for their marriage.

Maybe you know someone whose marriage has fallen apart. Perhaps they're watching to see if you will work out your problems and arguments. Or will you end your marriage, as well? We can show them that their marriage can be healed. They can be helped.

Sometimes the best way to help your spouse and help them heal is to simply listen. Maybe they just want you to listen and not fix anything. If your marriage isn't cold or hot, there's one other alternative—lukewarm.

LUKEWARM is usually not the first option for most people. The truth is that it's a far cry from the best. It's middle of the ground, settling for mediocrity. Sadly, like the church in this passage, many marriages succumb to this temperature. Notice Jesus' response to the church that wasn't refreshing and invigorating to others. Look at what He said to them because people weren't being helped by them and consequently were looking to other things to heal the pain of their problems. Their lukewarmness made Him want to vomit! He wanted to throw up.

I know your works; you are neither cold nor hot.
Would that you were either cold or hot!
REVELATION 3:15

Could He say the same about our marriages? Sadly, in many marriages, the answer is "yes." The most important human in our lives deserves our best, yet unfortunately, we often give them mediocre effort. God wants to vomit at our vain attempts to coast through our marriages and not treat them as the critical relationship He created them to be.

We began our marriage by stating in our vows that we would die for our spouse. And yet now we care more about the promotions and status than we do their feelings. We say they matter more to us than anyone else, but we can't make it home for dinner due to working late. It's funny how people we *aren't even* married to get the most and the best of our time. Even with our spouses, we're often distracted by the text, tweet, email, post, or gigantic list of things that must be done before the next day.

This is why Jesus wants to vomit over our marriages. He's sick and tired of everyone and everything getting the best of us at the expense of our relationship with Him and our spouses. Chances are your marriage is now lukewarm, has been lukewarm in the past, or is heading there even now. If so, there is a remedy. We can experience a marriage that is refreshing again. Our marriages can be places of help and healing again. How? The answer is given in verse 19! Be enthusiastic and repent!

> *We can experience a marriage that is refreshing again.*

> *Those whom I love, I reprove and discipline, so be zealous and repent.*
> REVELATION 3:19 (ESV)

Be excited about the times your marriage was cold or hot. Be enthusiastic about the potential for it to be that way again. Excitement about something breeds action to make it happen. To "repent" means to change direction and change your mind. The Amplified Bible takes it a step further and says it means to change your old way of thinking—your sinful behavior.

So basically, it means that we involve God in the process. When we understand and admit that God's desire for our marriage has not been achieved by us and we have been allowing mediocrity to dominate our spouses, it should cause us to want to change. He wants good things for us!

God wants our marriages to thrive! He cares deeply about you and your spouse! He died for you and them. His desire to give us a refreshing, invigorating, healing, helpful marriage should turn us from our mediocre, dull, and lukewarm marriages. We must confess that we've messed up His plan and ask Him to forgive and restore. Your marriage is one turn away from being the temperature God wants it to be!

He won't force His way! God is a gentleman and will only go where He's invited. He can do more with your marriage than you can. You can't change on your own, but He can change you and your marriage. It starts with Him because marriage was His idea in the first place. He created you and your spouse perfectly and specifically for each other.

If you want the marriage of your dreams, do it His way. Give Him your marriage! Repent. Admit you messed up His plan and design for your marriage, and ask Him to restore your marriage to His plan. Be ready when you pray this, though.

To change your marriage, He will want to change you as well. If you let Him change *you,* your marriage will change. Maybe you ask Him to give you the courage to stop giving your best to others and start giving it to your spouse. Perhaps you ask Him to show you the areas in your life that keep your marriage from being hot or cold. Repent from your mediocre lukewarm marriage!

Your spouse and your marriage deserve your best—not the cheap imitation we've been content with giving them. Stop making God vomit. Make Him proud. Bring refreshment and invigoration back to your marriage. Let Him heal and help so you and your spouse can get the healing and help needed. You will be glad you did!

— Taking a Minute for Your Marriage

Healing a wounded marriage isn't easy. It takes the Lord's help to change the tone or environment in your home. Try some of these simple changes to repent or to change the direction of a lukewarm relationship:

- *Turn off your cell phone when you come home from work.*
- *Instead of watching TV, choose something interactive, like a game, to relax with your spouse in the evening. Just don't get too competitive!*
- *Leave compliments or words of affection on sticky notes around the house.*
- *Laugh often to bring good medicine into your relationship.*

CHAPTER 14

THIRSTY MARRIAGE

HAVE YOU EVER thought about what makes you thirsty? Of course, we are not doctors or experts on how body science works. But speaking from experience, there are times when we get thirsty and specific reasons for it. These same reasons can cause your marriage to become parched. And any thirst which isn't quenched will leave us unfulfilled and searching for something to satisfy it. So what are the reasons our marriages become thirsty?

The first is **CONSTANT CHATTERING.** We become thirsty because we talk too much. Whether trying to prove a point, exerting our knowledge on topics, or simply voicing our opinions, Jon and Teresa talk—and we talk a lot! To the extent that our throats get dry and we get thirsty.

Your spouse may be the thirsty one in your marriage. Maybe they had a hard day and want to discuss it with you. However, you've been so busy talking that they can't feel like they can convey their feelings. Maybe they're thirsting for attention, but you're constantly talking to people at work or on the phone, spending time on a hobby, or binge-watching a show.

Either your marriage will die of thirst, or it will be filled by someone or something else. The Bible says we should be slow to speak. God gave us more ears than mouths; maybe that's a sign that we should use more of what we have. Listen more, chatter less!

Secondly, we get thirsty due to **CIRCUMSTANCES.** If it's hot, we want water to quench our thirst. Sometimes when it's cold outside, we get a coffee to warm us up. It's mealtime, so we need something to drink while we eat. We often ingest liquid based on what's going on or the circumstances.

You and your spouse may thirst for that new car or bigger home because the conditions say you should have it, and other couples are splurging on these things. Your spouse hurts you, so your thirst to be loved and appreciated rages. So you start clicking, surfing, or texting only to find out that the bad image you pull up online or that coworker who "gets" you won't quench your thirst. They will only make you thirst more. You know you can't handle it, but you give in and drink anyway.

Maybe you thirst to have the life other couples portray on social media—one that appears free from drama and stress. To quench this thirst, you obsess about how to make yourselves look better to the world. So, you crash diet, volunteer for everything you can, and post accolades everywhere, only to discover that the thirst to be noticed isn't quenched. That's because there's always someone in the social media realm that's got it more together than you. Your thirst to be noticed could be quenched simply by you and your spouse paying attention to each other again. God gave you each other.

Stop trying to be a hero to the world and be a hero to your spouse. Throughout Scripture, countless tales are told of the Israelites following every trend, fad, and god that was popular at the time. Their thirst wasn't quenched because they kept bouncing around. The circumstances dictated what or whom they thirsted after. Only when they were at rock bottom and defeated did they run back to the Lord and find what they were looking for.

Let's not use them as a model! Know that your thirst can only be quenched by Jesus. He said those who follow Him will be satisfied. When He quenches your thirst, you can be like the apostle Paul and say, "I am content no matter the situation." When you're content through Jesus, you will be satisfied with your marriage and have no need to have your thirst filled by the world, or its circumstances.

Finally, we thirst because of the **CROWD**. Picture this: You're headed somewhere with other people, but you stop to fill up. While there, they get a drink, and suddenly you do, too, even if you didn't realize you were thirsty. If others are grabbing sodas or water at gatherings, you don't want to look bad, so you do, too. We all do this. Others' opinions are a big deal to us. Your marriage and what happens (or doesn't) may be based on others you hang out with and talk to.

Keeping up with the Joneses is prevalent, prominent, and powerful in today's culture. But that line of thinking is ruining marriages. We want to be liked. We want to be noticed. The problem is that we seek this from the wrong people.

We exist for an audience of one; that one is God. Therefore, what He says about you and your spouse should matter more than what anyone else says or thinks.

I praise you, for I am fearfully and wonderfully made.
PSALM 139:14

Since God doesn't base our worth and value on the car we drive, the house we live in, or how successful we are, we shouldn't thirst after what everyone else says matters.

1 Kings 18 has a remarkable story about how influential the thirst to be like everyone else is. Basically, there's one guy, a prophet named Elijah, who stands alone for God. He challenges the people he knows and loves to a showdown: Choose the false gods they

thirst after but never get satisfaction from, or choose the one and only true God that gives life, freedom, and joy.

Elijah even makes a powerful statement when he asks, "How long will you hesitate between two opinions? If the Lord is God, then follow Him. But if it's Baal (*these other things we thirst after*), then follow him."

The people were so addicted to being cool and fitting in with the crowd that they followed and copied whatever everyone else did. If you read further in the story, you'll find that they end up empty and defeated as the god they thirsted for didn't answer or respond and did nothing for them!

Sadly, we can all be like the people in Elijah's day. We can have lives and marriages empty and void of power and vitality when we chase and thirst after the crowd and what they do. However, your marriage *can* be different. Instead of thirsting for the things that everyone else in the world does, you can experience satisfaction, fulfillment, joy, and life. Incidentally, the things of this world typically leave you empty, unfulfilled, and often seeking relief through a divorce, affairs, and addictions.

Perhaps your marriage is hanging on by a thread; don't be like the crowd and bolt. Stand and fight. Recommit to God and to each other. Be okay with who you're with. Be content with where God has you. And know that He has a plan to prosper you and give you a hope and a future. Our thirst will never be quenched if we constantly try to be like everyone else.

Just because everyone else does it, doesn't mean you have to.

Our marriages are unique and special. You are not supposed to be anyone else but yourself. Your spouse isn't just that guy or that gal; they are who God made them to be. Resolve in your heart to be okay with this.

The grass isn't always greener elsewhere! Just because everyone else does it, doesn't mean you have to. Stop the constant chatter and listen instead. Don't let circumstances cause you to sip from worldly things that won't satisfy you. Refuse to let the crowd influence you. You and your marriage can and should be different. Let's ensure that we do everything we can to ensure our thirst (and our spouses' thirst) is satisfied by Jesus and each other! We will be glad we did!

 — Taking a Minute for Your Marriage

Have you ever been lost in a crowd of people? You feel pushed and pulled in a common direction, and you may not even know where you're headed. Life can be like that. We imitate others, seek their approval, and unfortunately, we become parched because these actions never satisfy us. The opinions of others cannot quench our need to be loved. Only God can.

Where do you need God's refreshing touch today? Are you caught up in a situation or circumstance where you feel lost in the crowd? Ask for guidance as you recommit your marriage to the Lord.

CHAPTER 15

TRIANGULAR MARRIAGE

TRIANGLES ARE interesting. Toddlers learn about this vital shape early in life. But triangles also serve adults as tools in mathematics, construction design, and even as musical instruments. Within the context of marriage, triangles remind of the intent of marriage from its creation and illustrate the power of not just two but three people delicately entwined. Without the three entities working in cohesion, the triangle would not be complete. It would not even be a triangle. Using the triangle analogy, we will see how our marriages can be infused with abundant power to last until death, hope to make it through hard times, and love that endures.

Ecclesiastes 4:12 paints the picture of a cord with three strands united. Picture the strands forming a triangle with God at the top, you and your spouse at the bottom, one on each side. Now imagine the bottom line represents the two connecting to one another in a horizontal relationship. And each line going to the top represents each of you linking to God vertically.

Ideally, this is how marriage should look. Solomon, the wisest and richest man of his generation, said that when these parts are connected together, it's hard to break them apart. So how do we make sure all sides are connecting well?

The first way is through the **SPOUSAL CONNECTION.** According to Dictionary.com, the word *connection* is "something that communicates or relates" or "a person who helps another achieve a goal." Both definitions are perfect in describing a healthy, vibrant marriage relationship.

When we connect with our spouses, we communicate with and relate to them thoroughly. Conversation flows freely. Feelings are validated, and each person feels loved, valued, honored, and respected. But, unfortunately, many times, our connection with our spouse can get disturbed.

Just like we can lose a picture on TV when a storm hits, we can lose our relationship with our spouse immediately or gradually over time. Bitterness, resentment, and unforgiveness are some of the many ways our spousal connection can be damaged. Maybe you're secretly hiding something. Perhaps you haven't been entirely trustworthy with your spouse, or maybe they hurt you, and you've become distant from them because you have not dealt with it. Is there anything causing a barrier between you and your spouse that is affecting communication and connection?

Notice the second definition: "One person who helps another achieve a goal." As we get older and years go by, we become content with not setting goals and just living day-by-day. When you got married, was there something that you wanted to do? Was there an experience you and your spouse hoped to partake in? Even now, are you setting new goals each year? Is your marriage better now than when you first married?

If not, it may be because your connection is off. Instead of working together to achieve your marital goals, outside influences and the rigors of daily living have caused you to put those goals on a shelf. For example, maybe you dream of being healthier to be fit enough to enjoy doing things together as a couple.

Have you and your spouse worked together to help accomplish that goal? When our connection is off with our spouse, our goals will not be achieved, and our communication and relatability will be severely hindered. On the other hand, we can relate to, communicate effectively with, and help our spouse achieve goals if we get our connection right. That may mean we need to overhaul some areas in our own lives.

Maybe we spend less time watching shows and more time laughing together. Perhaps you and your spouse need a date night or a weekend away where it's just the two of you. Maybe you need to say I'm sorry and ask for forgiveness. Whatever could hinder your connection with your spouse has to be discarded for harmony to return to your marriage. This and every other horizontal relationship will be out of whack if our vertical relationship with God is disconnected, bringing us to the next connection on the triangle.

Our **SPIRITUAL CONNECTION** is the most critical connection we will ever have. Every other relationship and connection in life flows through it. As we've said before, *God* created marriage. So it stands to reason that this connection involves God and what we do with Him. There are two integral pieces to ensure this connection is correct and helps make our spousal connection right. The first deals with eternity, and the second deals with the everyday. Both are vital and require a commitment. We will start with the eternal piece.

Our spiritual connection begins and ends with eternity. It involves **saying "yes" to God.** Maybe you're wondering what you need to say "yes" to. First, ponder these questions: Do you know right from wrong? Would you agree that certain truths are relevant and valid for all? For instance, murder and theft are punishable by law anywhere you go. Those that break the law are subject to punishment for that crime.

These two concrete truths didn't just come about. Someone had to set the standard that labels right from wrong. That someone was God. He sets the bar. He determines right from wrong. He even gave a standard for us live by—The Ten Commandments. Maybe you say, "Well, I haven't murdered anyone or stolen anything."

But have you lied? Have you coveted something another person owned, like a car? A home? Have you said something about someone that wasn't true and would damage their character? These examples, and others, are part of the list of commandments. Yet *none* of us—not one—has adhered to them. In fact, James writes in his letter that breaking *one* of the ten commandments is the same as breaking them *all*. James also said you violate the standard God has set if you know what's right to do and don't do it. So saying "yes" starts with acknowledging that you have a problem with sin, that you've broken God's standard for living.

Once you admit you have a problem, you have to say "yes" to the fact that punishment must result from the infraction committed. The sin must be atoned for. The guilty must pay the penalty. The penalty we deserve for breaking God's law is eternal separation from Him in a place called Hell.

Hell is a place the Bible denotes as a place of agony, torment, and complete separation from God. Though we deserve this judgment, God, out of immense love for us, sent His Son, Jesus Christ, to earth to live the life we should've lived. He's the only person that never violated God's standards or broke His commandments.

But He didn't come just to live a perfect life and make us feel bad that we couldn't. Instead, He came to pay the penalty for our sins. He died on the cross to satisfy God's standard for restitution. The book of Hebrews says without the shedding of blood, there is no forgiveness of sin. He died so that instead of eternal separation from God in Hell, we could have eternal fellowship with God in Heaven. His death gives us life, and we don't have to do anything to earn it because we can't.

It is by grace through faith that we are saved, not by works so that no one can boast.
EPHESIANS 2:8-9

The wages of sin is death but the free gift of God is eternal life through Jesus Christ our Lord.
ROMANS 6:23

We can't earn it, but we can have this gift by saying "yes" to Jesus and His death for our sins! Once you do this, you enter into a relationship with God. You are guaranteed Heaven forever, and you're changed and can live daily with new passion, purpose, and meaning. That brings us to the second aspect of the spiritual connection.

Once we say "yes" to God for an eternal relationship, we need to **spend quality time with God.** This has a significant impact on our everyday relationships, especially our marriages. Spending time with God can be done in several ways. First, find a Bible translation you can understand. Then as you read it, memorize and highlight verses that stick out to you.

There are many plans to help you do this. But to make things easy, begin with the book of John to get a picture of God's love for you. Or read a chapter of Proverbs daily. In doing so, you will have read an entire book of the Bible in approximately one month.

The Bible helps us with daily struggles and gives us wisdom and encouragement to make it day by day. Discuss with your spouse what God revealed to you through your scripture reading. The more time you spend in His Word, the more you will become like Him—and the more it will help your marriage. Make studying His Word a priority, and make sure the time you devote to it is away from distractions and interruptions.

Another powerful way to spend time with God is through prayer, simply talking to God. He already knows what's going on with you.

But like a friend or family member, He wants to hear from and communicate with you. As you're praying, listen to what He says. The relationship should be a two-way relationship.

Don't just pray and ask God to bless your food or life. Don't use prayer as an outlet to try to get God to bail you out of a situation you've gotten yourself into. Make it your first response, not your last resort. In prayer, allow God to reveal anything hindering your relationship with Him and your spouse. When He does, ask and invite Him to change you. Pray with and for your spouse. Ask God to protect your marriage and use it for His glory! Pray that He would make you the spouse your partner wants and desires.

Ask God to protect your marriage and use it for His glory!

Additionally, we can spend quality time with God by actively attending and serving in a Bible-believing and proclaiming church. Don't let other things get in the way. When you become actively involved in a church, you will realize that others experience the same struggles and life issues as you. Attending and serving with your spouse in worship, small groups, and other church activities will strengthen your marriage.

You can do many things together as a couple but being in church is one of the most vital for the overall health of your marriage. God can use you and your spouse to help other couples in their relationship. You need the ministry of a church, and the church needs your gifts, talents, and abilities to effectively minister to others. Perhaps you and your spouse can help and reach people that others in the church can't assist.

By actively participating in the ministry of a local church, you're also giving your children a solid foundation that will pay huge dividends in their future. Children often choose to follow their parents' customs and beliefs. If you make time with God a priority in your marriage, there's a great chance that your children will do the same in theirs.

If your spiritual connection is out of whack, every other relationship in life will also be. Maybe all your marriage needs is a concerted effort to strengthen and reinforce your relationship with God. Even if you've never read the Bible or attended church before, you can start today. Your prayer life may be regulated to meal time or crises, but that can also change.

In the triangle, God is at the top. This is because our relationship with Him should be the most important of our lives. Maybe you've never said "yes" to God, being guaranteed Heaven as a result. You can do that simply by reciting "A, B, C."

- **Admit** you're a sinner. Agree with the fact that you've broken God's standard and law.
- **Believe** that Jesus' death on the cross is enough to satisfy God's required punishment for sin. Ask Him to forgive you of sin, come into your life and change you.
- **Commit** to Him as the Lord of your life. Commit to living your life for Him and ask for His help.

Take the first step in showing that you're committed to Him by being baptized as an outward sign of an inward change. Ask Him to help your marriage honor and glorify Him. Ask Him for a desire to read and understand His Word. Commit to prayer and active participation in a church. Make the cord of three strands hard to break by ensuring your connections are not hindered or disconnected. God and our spouses are the two most important relationships we will ever have. Let's keep them that way by keeping our spiritual and spousal connections flowing freely!

 — *Taking a Minute for Your Marriage*

This chapter mentioned the similarities between marriage and a simple triangle. God is at the top of the triangle's apex, and we are at

the adjacent corners. Complete the following exercise on a separate piece of paper:

1. Draw a triangle as illustrated below, inserting your names.
2. In the middle of the triangle, write a verse representing a promise from God that you and your spouse are standing together for.
3. Place this drawing in a prominent place in your home, where you will continually be reminded of God's word for you.

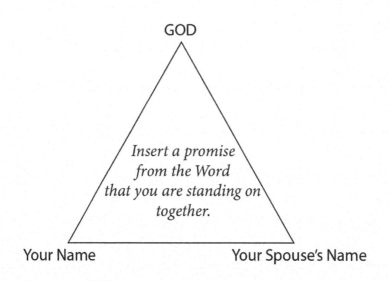

GOD

Insert a promise from the Word that you are standing on together.

Your Name   Your Spouse's Name

CHAPTER 16

TOUGHNESS

FORMER PASTOR AND AUTHOR Robert Schuller wrote a book called *"Tough Times Never Last, But Tough People Do!"* This statement is true and can help us in our marriages. If we commit to three integral pieces tucked into Schuller's title, we will find that lifelong marriage is possible. These pieces and our understanding of them can provide us with the stick-to-it-ive·ness necessary to truly remain married until death. We pray and hope that as we dissect each of the three pieces, we all will come away with a greater commitment to lifelong marriages.

Notice the first part of the title: *Tough times don't last.* So the first precept we see here is that there is a **PROMISE.** The promise is that times will be tough. It's vitally important to understand this so we can prepare. Not everything in marriage will be sunshine and roses, Hallmark movies, and easy street. It will be hard. There will be struggles. The concept of transitioning from thinking about or looking out for ourselves only to adding another person into the equation can make some cringe.

Just as the Titanic sank due to lack of preparation and adjustments, marriages can shipwreck and sink because often, we are not prepared for rough seas and hard times; therefore, we don't know how to adjust. I Corinthians 7:28 implies that those who marry will have troubles. Nothing worth having is ever easy.

Yet so many marriages crumble because spouses go into it thinking it will be a piece of cake. After all, they're in love. You are promised hard times. It will happen because all of us sin. No one aside from Jesus is perfect.

Have you ever experienced something you weren't adequately prepared for? Be it a test, a job interview, a meeting, or something else, we could all agree that the anxiety and stress caused by the unpreparedness were something we vividly remember and don't want to experience again!

That's why we must know hard times will come in marriage and prepare accordingly. Talk with your spouse and plan how to handle situations or crises when they arise. If you're engaged or dating someone, prepare now for hard times. Make sure you're not blindsided and willing to pack up and leave when they happen. Remember, the hard times won't last forever, but your marriage can.

The second nugget we get from this title is **PERSISTENCE.** As a synonym for "tough," this word brings excellent stories to mind. From Edison's hundred-plus times in failing to create the light bulb, or Abraham Lincoln facing political and family loss before being elected president, to the great fictional heroes like Rocky Balboa and The Little Engine That Could, we all can recall people who have persisted to success. And we know of those who have quit, full of regret and unfulfilled hopes and dreams.

Everyone who makes it has to persist!

"*Tough people do*" is the next part of the title. Are you tough? Is your marriage tough? Would you and your spouse survive if tragedy, betrayal, secrecy, or another bomb exploded in your marriage? Would you persist? Would things last?

Everyone who makes it *has* to persist! Anyone can quit. Anyone can throw in the towel. But only the tough press on and stay the course.

And let us run with perseverance [persistence] the race marked out for us.
HEBREWS 12:1

Exercise is challenging, but it's worth it. It hurts, but we stay at it. So many people work long hours until retirement and run themselves ragged. If we can persist in these areas, we can keep our marriages together.

The third piece to the puzzle of toughness is the **POWER OF DO**. Notice the title says that tough people "do." That involves action. And it is action now and action in the future. In other words, continual action. We must take action to make our marriage work. It's a present and future action. What we do today will affect the future.

What can you do today that will impact the future of your marriage and family? Will you forgive? Will you stay committed to working it out? Will you choose to struggle with them as opposed to living without them? Will you serve your spouse?

Love is a verb. Will you date your spouse? Doing involves moving. You can sit back and do nothing and let your marriage suffer and end, or you can do something. Your marriage and your future are hanging in the balance.

Decide today to be tough. Toughness is hard; so many in the world have become soft and lack toughness because it's hard. When we understand the promise that things will be hard, persist without exception and use the power of "do," our marriages will be stronger and healthier than ever.

— Taking a Minute for Your Marriage

Life isn't linear. There are always ups and downs as we move through it. Can you recall a time in your marriage when you faced a challenge that had to be overcome?

What was the outcome? Did that situation make you stronger? Was your resiliency increased because of it?

Ask the Lord to give you wisdom and guidance as you and your spouse face tough times in the future. Use the overcoming opportunities from your past to persevere through life's challenges in the days to come.

SECTION 4

AVOIDING TORPEDOES IN YOUR MARRIAGE

CHAPTER 17

TORPEDO #1
COMPARISON

TORPEDOES ARE EXPLOSIVE DEVICES used in naval battles to destroy and ruin opponents. In fact, the word torpedo in verb form means to destroy, demolish, and devastate. Just like boats, warships, submarines, and other naval devices can be destroyed by these devices, some torpedoes can damage, destroy, and even kill marriages. The following chapters will be devoted to identifying and combatting these torpedoes so they don't ruin our marriages. Though explosive and potentially destructive, these torpedoes can only cause destruction if they are launched. More often than not, we shoot these torpedoes at our spouses without thinking about the explosive consequences they could cause.

The first torpedo that destroys marriage is **COMPARISON**. Intentionally or unintentionally, we constantly compare ourselves to others. Whether it's body type, complexion, house size, car style, clothing, etc., we measure ourselves against others.

In marriage, it's no different; we are often guilty of saying, "why can't he or she be more like so and so?" Or "If only my wife kept the house clean as his wife does, things would be better." Or even, "I wish my husband had a job like her husband, so we could live in a bigger and better home." Bottom line—comparison kills and destroys.

If we love our spouse, like we say we do, we will refrain from comparing them to others. This is because the enemy wants us to feel shortchanged and be so discontent with what we have that we compare it with others. Comparison does one of two things: It makes us prideful, which leads to a fall, as the Bible says, or it makes us feel bad about ourselves.

In Psalm 8:5 and Hebrews 2:7, we're told that God created us "a little lower than the angels." So if we understand how God sees us and trust Him, we won't be as eager to compare ourselves with others. Do you compare yourself and your spouse to others? Do you find yourself agitated and aggravated about what you don't have that others do?

> *Let your spouse be themselves and be okay with it.*

If so, trust the Lord and rest in how He sees you and your spouse. He sees us all the same way. This means in His eyes, we're all on equal footing. Though we should value everyone, we don't want to compare ourselves to anyone. Be yourself. Let your spouse be themselves and be okay with it.

One of the best ways to ensure that the explosive torpedo of comparison doesn't cause irreparable damage to your marriage is to simply refuse to compare yourself and your spouse to anyone else. We're not saying we shouldn't desire and work to improve. But while we're working on bettering ourselves, we can remain content and appreciative of how God created our spouse and us. He doesn't make mistakes; by comparing ourselves to others, we are essentially saying He doesn't know what He's doing or has messed up. Your marriage is *your* marriage; it's not someone else's.

You will experience things that others won't. You may struggle in areas others don't. Your marriage may be healthier than others. Regardless of where your marriage is, it can be better. But ultimately, it's yours and no one else's.

Don't let the torpedo of comparison sink your marriage! Don't let it blow your marriage up and cause a loss of trust, passion, and love.

 — Taking a Minute for Your Marriage

Studies show that comparing yourself to others can lead to depression, low self-esteem, envy, and low self-confidence. Those aren't the qualities you should bring to a relationship! Have you ever found yourself comparing something in your marriage to that of another couple's marriage?

Here are three solutions to change the torpedo of comparison:

- ***Recognize*** *the dangers of comparison. Identify the area(s) where you typically keep an internal scorecard of comparison with others and consider how detrimental this can be to your relationship.*
- *Ask the Lord to **reveal** areas where you can better yourself by accepting who you are and what God has given you.*
- ***Resolve*** *to love your spouse more genuinely by acknowledging who they are and how they complete you.*

CHAPTER 18

TORPEDO #2 COMFORT ZONE

WE CONTINUE our look at explosive torpedoes that destroy marriages. Once detonated, these torpedoes leave irreparable damage and, like shrapnel, have lasting effects on a marriage. Unfortunately, the torpedo we will examine today is no different. In fact, it's common in many marriages and brings resentment, hostility, prolonged unhappiness, and stale marriages. Sadly, both husband and wife use this torpedo many times without realizing or acknowledging it; many relationships find themselves in the middle of this dangerous spot.

It's the comfort zone. Ultimately, it's the path of least resistance. But, unfortunately, it's the precursor to boredom. When boredom in marriage sets in, spouses go from being soulmates to roommates.

We marvel at people who accomplish great things. But here's the thing: For each monumental feat to have been achieved, a risk was taken, and the comfort zone had to be left. Even in Scripture, we can see how lives were changed by Jesus when the comfort zone was abandoned.

For instance, Zacchaeus did two uncharacteristic things to see Jesus. He was wealthy and well-known, yet he took risks. First, we read in Luke 19:4 that he runs and then climbs a tree. These two things were not condoned for a person of wealth and notoriety. In fact, if someone did either of these, people would be talking negatively about you later.

But Zacchaeus' desire for what he wanted was more significant than his desire to stay comfortable. He wasn't worried about what the people would say if he ran or climbed a tree. Because of the immense crowd surrounding Jesus and his short stature, he couldn't see Jesus, yet he refused to be deterred. His life was changed that day because he was willing to get uncomfortable.

Are you? Is harmony in your marriage important enough to you to risk saying, "I'm sorry?" Will you get uncomfortable and set limits on how much you work, for your marriage?

Every incredible feat or accomplishment comes when the comfort zone is left.

Maybe you've become bored in your marriage because you and your spouse are doing the same thing, the same way, day in and day out. It's been said that the definition of insanity is doing the same thing repeatedly and expecting a different result. Maybe you're expecting your spouse to cater to your every desire and whim, but you're unwilling to serve and do things for them. Perhaps routine consistent date nights will take your marriage from its comfort zone to thriving.

Yes, you will have to risk coming home from work early. You may need to go without Starbucks or a meal out and paying for a babysitter. But remember that the risk will produce a reward. The reward of a happier thriving non-boring marriage will far outweigh the risks we take to get out of the comfort zone that enabled those things.

Every incredible feat or accomplishment comes when the comfort zone is left. Every great, long-lasting marriage has two spouses committed to not letting stagnation, boredom, and humdrum attitudes and actions characterize them. They strive for more. Both husband and wife continually push themselves and risk popularity, funny looks, and their desires to ensure that the torpedo of the comfort zone doesn't blow up their marriage.

If Zacchaeus had never left his comfort zone, there's a great chance he would never have encountered Jesus. This would've meant that his life would never have been changed for the better. What if you don't leave the comfort zone of familiarity or how you've always done it? Will your marriage be any different? It can be. The choice is yours.

Suppose the saying is true that familiarity breeds contempt. In that case, it could be that you or your spouse is harboring contempt for the other because you're too used to each other. If it's been a while since you were wowed by your spouse, the torpedo of comfort zone has likely been launched.

You can head it off by not waiting for your spouse to change but by *you* changing. Schedule the date. Do something unique and unexpected for them. Help them with chores without being asked. Your marriage can be destroyed, or it can be different. The choice is yours!

 — Taking a Minute for Your Marriage

Marriage brings many excellent opportunities to break out of our comfort zone. But often, like Zacchaeus, we must make ourselves vulnerable to the reactions of others (namely, our spouses) by choosing not to remain comfortable in our daily routines.

Make a list of the things that make you "uncomfortable." List situations or scenarios where you feel awkward or uneasy about moving out of an area that is safe and familiar. Discuss a few of the items on the list with your spouse. Seek reassurance that it's ok to release your faith in moving toward a new accomplishment or achievement.

CHAPTER 19

TORPEDO #3 CONCEALMENT

PERHAPS NO OTHER torpedo stifles and hurts marriages like the one we will discuss today. Unlike other torpedoes that can be easily seen and detected, this one, at its very core, is about avoidance, hiding, and shadows. It's the torpedo of concealment and is waging war on marriages everywhere. Yet, because of its nature and the supposed ease of use, it's become an everyday "go-to" in many relationships and homes. Moreover, technology makes this torpedo's accessibility even more effortless.

Secrets, hiding destructive vices, and withholding feelings are all key to launching this devastating weapon. Rest assured that the unknown, the deception, the hidden things will be revealed. In fact, Jesus Himself said in Luke 8:17 that the secret things (the things we try to conceal) will come to light. They will be exposed.

> *For nothing is hidden that will not be made manifest, nor is anything secret that will not be known and come to light.*
> LUKE 8:17 (ESV)

The harsh reality is that when they are exposed to our spouse, the damage will be catastrophic, especially if they are exposed shockingly or unexpectedly. So how do we limit the damage? How do we avoid severe problems? The following tips will help us.

The first is **CONFESSION**. In our culture, confessing and owning up to our mistakes and faults is not something we do. The blame game sets in. Instead of taking responsibility for our fallacies, we focus on what others do or don't do. Owning up to our issues and making amends through confession is powerful. It puts us in right standing with God and others. 1 John 1:9 states, "if we confess our sins, He is faithful and just to forgive us our sins and cleanse us from all unrighteousness." So confession brings us back into right fellowship and standing with God. It also helps us with each other. James 5:16 encourages us to confess our sins to one another and pray for one another that we may be healed. When we confess to our spouse, our marriages are healed and made new. Maybe you need to confess some bitterness or animosity that's led to distance and aloofness in your marriage. Marriage counseling can also be helpful and can steer you in the right direction.

Secondly, to help our marriages with the torpedo of concealment, we must **COMMIT** to openness and transparency. One of the greatest ways to ensure this torpedo doesn't destroy our marriages is to commit to transparency above all else. Refuse to allow secrets and concealing things to be a part of your marriage. Give your spouse access to your technology. Don't withhold your feelings. Don't let something you need to deal with destroy your marriage. Refuse to do anything in secret. Let your spouse know what you're doing and what's bothering you. Help can't come if the issue isn't acknowledged.

> *Help can't come if the issue isn't acknowledged.*

The third tip to help is to **COME TOGETHER.** We aren't meant to do life alone. God wired us for relationships. It's genuinely easier to do something when others help. For example, in our home, exercising and eating right is much easier when both of us do it.

Alignment is key. Coming together and working with each other lessens the likelihood of a torpedo of concealment hitting your marriage. We need each other. Your spouse needs you.

Two people working together can accomplish great things. Whereas isolation allows secrecy and concealment to permeate, coming together greatly minimizes it and enables us to enjoy freedom and harmony in marriage. Remember that what is done in secret will be revealed. So save yourself and your spouse the heartache and pain, and don't allow the torpedo of concealment to destroy your marriage!

 — Taking a Minute for Your Marriage

Sometimes we believe hiding something from our spouse is in their best interest. Particularly if it is something from our past or from a time before we knew them. But when we give ourselves totally and entirely to our partner in marriage, we become one with each other and solidify trust in our relationship.

Is there something you haven't been upfront about with your spouse? Trust the Lord to show you the right time and give you the right words as you open yourself to them. Use your spiritual intuition to recognize the right opportunity to share your heart. Speak the truth and reaffirm your love and commitment to your relationship. Don't fear what you will lose by doing this. Instead, embrace what you will gain in deciding that there will be no secrets in your marriage.

SECTION 5

A TOTAL TRANSPLANT OF THE H.E.A.R.T.

CHAPTER 20

TRANSPLANT "H" HONOR

OVER THE NEXT few chapters, we will discuss how to have a thriving marriage by giving your marriage a **H.E.A.R.T.** transplant. Together we will discover and understand the things we must transplant into our marriages to obtain the optimal desired results. We chose the acronym h.e.a.r.t. because our heart is key to life and well-being. The qualities we share are central to the health and well-being of our marriage.

HONOR is the first key to a marriage heart transplant that yields a thriving marriage. To honor someone means to esteem or respect them. Literally, it means to regard highly. How highly do you regard your spouse? Are they esteemed more than anyone or anything else? Romans 12:10 challenges us to "outdo one another in showing honor."

We live in a society where everyone wants to outdo each other. One-up-man-ship has become second nature. Think about how much priority is placed on achieving more than someone else or accumulating more than others. Imagine how much better our marriages would be if, instead of trying to outdo everyone else in stuff, we made it our mission to outdo our spouse in honoring them. To do this, we must regard them highly in three areas.

The first is our **TIME**. When you look at your day, how highly esteemed would your spouse feel with the amount of quality time they receive from you? Do you call them on your lunch break to let them know you're thinking about them? Do you take time to listen to your spouse when they've had a stressful or demanding day? Or do you come in from work and just plop down on the couch to veg out? Are you more concerned about "me" time or the plans your friends have for you? Is your spouse getting your leftovers in the area of time?

The second way we can honor our spouses is with our **TALENTS**. You and your spouse are likely different in at least one, if not many, ways. This means that you have talents your spouse doesn't. Maybe you are creative and artistic. If so, paint, draw, or sculpt something for your spouse that will honor them. Perhaps you are a tremendous cook. Use that talent to celebrate your spouse with a surprise meal with their favorite food. Maybe you are talented with words. Write a poem or song and read or sing it to your spouse. To honor them, we have to be willing to take action.

God has given you gifts and talents that he wants you to use as a gift to others, especially your spouse. Maybe you are reading this thinking that you are pretty dull. Or that you're not as talented as someone else. Both of those lines of thought are wrong and filled with lies. Because you were uniquely created, you have talents and abilities given explicitly to you to honor your spouse. It's easy to say we will do these things. However, it's harder to take the necessary action to make that happen when we get caught up in giving the best of our focus and energy to many other people and things. Your spouse needs and yearns for honor; use your talents to meet that need.

Your spouse needs and yearns for honor; use your talents to meet that need.

The third area in which we can show honor to our spouses is our **TREASURE**. We would all probably agree that it takes money and resources to function and live in today's world. Sadly for most people, after paying their bills, there isn't much left to do anything special with or for their spouse. We are not saying that you should accrue a ton of debt. Instead, we advise that you find a way within your means and budget to spend money on your spouse. Sacrificing a meal out or a Starbucks drink might be an option. Maybe you could use the money you had planned for something for yourself and use it on a nice getaway or gift for your spouse. It doesn't have to be elaborate. Remember that if corporations and other institutions can honor retirees and employees with gifts, we can surely find ways to give gifts to our spouses.

Your spouse must know they are honored or esteemed more highly than anyone else. Make this a priority. Give your marriage a transplant of a heart that is brimming with honor. Work to outdo your spouse in the area of honor. Make it a regular occurrence and watch your marriage thrive the way it was intended to. You and your spouse deserve it!

 — Taking a Minute for Your Marriage

Honoring someone means thinking well of them and not trying to change them into someone else. This is carried out by both our words and our actions. Ask the Lord to give you a fresh and creative idea today that will help you honor your spouse. Make this a priority.

Before the sun sets tonight, creatively and lovingly express honor toward them. Here are a few ideas to get you started:
- *Pick up a cup of their favorite coffee.*
- *Bring home a bouquet of flowers.*
- *Rub their feet.*

- *Offer sincere appreciation for their effort to keep your home safe, secure, and well-maintained.*
- *Ask them about their day but turn off your phone and really listen to their response.*

CHAPTER 21

TRANSPLANT "E" ENCOURAGEMENT

THE SECOND AREA where our marriages may need a heart transplant is seldomly used but frequently needed—that is **ENCOURAGEMENT**. In fact, if you asked anyone, including your spouse, if they need encouragement, you will likely get an emphatic "yes" in reply. In today's world, it is needed now more than ever. Scripture is bursting with examples of the power that encouragement brings.

The first avenue of encouragement is in our **WORDS**. In Daniel 10:11, Daniel has an encounter with an angel. The angel calls Daniel a "man treasured by God." The angel repeats it in verse 19 and then encourages Daniel to be strong and have peace. We also find in verse 19 that these encouraging words strengthened Daniel. Likewise, we can strengthen and encourage our spouses through what we say. For example, when your spouse comes in from work, they need to be encouraged, not nagged. There might be a laundry list of things you need to talk to them about, but before you go right into that, make sure they are ready to hear it.

Chances are that they might have had a rough day at work and could really use an encouraging word from their spouse when they first get home. Ask them how their day was and truly listen to see how you might encourage them. Be supportive and take notice of what they are saying. Find ways to compliment their efforts even if the results aren't perfect. By your words, let them know that you value them and all they do for the family.

Another way we can infuse encouragement into our marriages is through the **WAY WE INTERACT** with each other. As vital as our words, this is just as important. Read the passage below from Philippians, as Paul provides guidelines for us to follow to do this:

> *Do nothing from selfish ambition or conceit, but in humility count others more significant than yourselves. Let each of you look not only to his own interests, but also to the interests of others. Have this mind among yourselves, which is yours in Christ Jesus, who, though he was in the form of God, did not count equality with God a thing to be grasped, but emptied himself, by taking the form of a servant, being born in the likeness of men. And being found in human form, he humbled himself by becoming obedient to the point of death, even death on a cross.*
>
> PHILIPPIANS 2:3-8

Paul says that we should take the focus off of ourselves and put it on others, especially our spouses. How do we do this? By thinking of them as more important than us. If we are completely honest, we will admit that we spend a lot of time thinking about ourselves and what we want. We think about what and where we want to eat. We think about what we're going to do when we get home, how great it will be to go to the deer camp for a weekend, and things like that.

In reality, these things aren't bad; it is natural to think about your own wants and needs. However, the scripture challenges us to think about others more than ourselves. This takes humility and self-sacrifice, two things that do not come naturally. Take time for an evaluation of yourself and your marriage. Maybe the bitterness and hostility you might be experiencing in your marriage stem from a spouse who feels like you only care about yourself and not them. Are your actions saying this?

However, maybe you are great at serving your spouse and putting their wishes ahead of yours. But what about when you're in a discussion or argument? Are you so selfish that you care more about your feelings than your spouse's? Do you allow them a chance to share how they are feeling? Or do you always feel the need to prove your point or provide a comeback?

Looking back at this passage, we see that Paul points us to Jesus. Though He had the right to demand allegiance and that everyone would see things His way, Jesus served and allowed them to choose how they responded. He consistently sacrificed His reputation, comfort, sleep, and scores of other personal needs for the well-being of others and their interests. Consequently, throngs of people followed Him then and still do today. The ultimate act of sacrifice was His death on the cross for the sins of all mankind.

You might think your spouse doesn't deserve you putting their interests ahead of yours. Because they may not help out around the house. Or they may be selfish and only think about themselves. They truly may not deserve your encouragement, shown through your selflessness. But that's precisely what Jesus did—even when *we* didn't deserve it.

When you and I didn't merit His love and sacrifice for our sins, He still willingly sacrificed His life. Isaiah 52:14 says that He was beaten so bad, He was unrecognizable! Imagine what that meant. Sacrificing His personal comfort. Leaving pain-free Heaven, Jesus came to Earth to experience the emotional pain of betrayal of friends, the physical pain of beatings and crucifixion, and the spiritual pain

When we feel like we can't, remember that through Him, we can!

of separation from His Father! He endured this even though we didn't deserve it.

That's why Paul points us to look to Him as an example of how to interact with others. We can put our spouses' needs above ours through Christ and His help. He can give us the ability and resources necessary to provide them with the encouragement they need, even if they don't deserve it! So when we feel like we can't, remember that through Him, we *can!*

 — Taking a Minute for Your Marriage

The word "encouragement" comes from combining two Old French words. First, "en," which means to intensely put yourself into something, and then "corage," which means to make strong and heartened. So when we en-courage, we put ourselves into the lives of others to make them strong.

Begin to express encouragement toward your spouse more deliberately. Share encouraging Scriptures with them. E.g., "Honey, I know you already know this, but the Bible says that when we raise our children in the knowledge of the Lord, they will not depart from it when they grow up. So someday, you'll be blessed by how our children honor God, even though it's been hard while they were young."

Or, tell your spouse something you really like about them, like:
- *"That color really brings out the depth of your beautiful eyes."*
- *"I feel so loved when you keep my clothes washed and put away."*
- *"I appreciate how you serve our family, and thank you for all you do."*

CHAPTER 22

TRANSPLANT "A" ACCEPTANCE

WE BELIEVE THIS TOPIC can become a root cause of divorce and broken marriages. When a marriage commences, this trait is very apparent and easily applied. However, this once-valued trait seems to wither as years go on. As we delve into this chapter, we pray that the characteristic of **ACCEPTANCE** will be rekindled and rejuvenated in your marriages so that joy, exuberance, and passion may return. Before you skip ahead or even put the book down, please consider if you have fallen into the trap of not accepting your spouse—entirely and totally.

In John, Chapter 4, a fascinating story unfolds that provides a better understanding of how to wholeheartedly accept our spouse and not get so easily frustrated or bitter toward them. Beginning in verse 5, we are told that Jesus arrives in a town and is exhausted. He had been traveling from town to town on foot, ministering to people, and was utterly worn out.

Jesus made His way to a well to get a drink at a part of the day when more than likely, it was hot enough that no one would be there to bother Him. Most people would have already drawn their daily water in the cool of the morning. However, Jesus was there in the heat of the day when he noticed a woman. She was not just any woman, though; she was a Samaritan. It was against Jewish law for Jesus to talk to such a woman. Samaritans were supposed to be despised, hated, and avoided at all costs by Jews. But Jesus flips the script.

As the story continues, we notice that the woman has a reputation. So she probably came to the well at this hot time of the day to avoid the remarks, glares, and comments that others would have made about her. Also, as a woman, she wasn't expecting a self-respecting man to pay attention to her. Let's see what Jesus does and how this applies to acceptance.

THE SIGNIFICANCE OF THE WOMAN AT THE WELL

First, we see that He accepted her as a **PERSON**. He didn't look at her the way others did. The labels that were placed on her didn't matter to Him. He saw her value as a person. He understood that she was broken and flawed and needed acceptance to find her desired freedom.

It's safe to say that she was looking for acceptance in relationships. Still, Jesus gave her what she wanted without strings attached. How about you? Do you see your spouse as a person who, like you, is broken and flawed? Are you willing to accept them and their shortcomings, knowing that acceptance of them as a person is more valuable to them than your correction?

Secondly, Jesus accepted her **PAST**. Continuing with verses 16-18, Jesus tells her to bring her husband into the conversation. The woman confesses that she wasn't married. After agreeing with that statement, Jesus adds to it by mentioning that she had previously been married five times and was now living with a guy she wasn't married to. When others would've condemned or shunned her because of this, Jesus accepted her.

Jesus instead accepted her.

He knew her past and still chose to accept her. Likewise, your spouse's past has likely shaped them into who they are today! This means that you have a choice to accept them despite their past and what they've done. Or, you can condemn them for it.

Jesus viewed this woman as redeemable. Your spouse isn't irredeemable. Their past doesn't have to determine your marriage's future. Are you holding something from your spouse's past against them? Is something from their past rendering them irredeemable? For the sake of your marriage, will you choose Jesus' example of acceptance over the world's example of condemnation?

When we are young and immature, many of us make choices that can later cause us great shame and regret. Also, there might have even been past relationships or addictions that your spouse had that they are still healing from. Accepting your spouse's past as part of their identity will allow you two to bond together to build a new future. Take time to be open and transparent with your spouse, so they can understand where you are coming from. They can help you heal or learn how to better relate to you in different situations if they know more about your past.

Accepting your spouse's past also means accepting that they may have a different view on things based on how they were raised. Learn to talk about your background, how your parents interacted with you, and what that taught you about marriage, parenting, work ethic, or finances. Then be accepting that this part of their upbringing affects how they relate to things in your marriage. If there are unhealthy habits, pray together for God to unite you on these matters so that your past does not hinder your future in marriage. For the sake of your marriage, will you choose Jesus' example of acceptance over the world's example of condemnation?

The third way Jesus accepted the woman at the well that applies to our marriages is that He accepted the **POWER TO CHANGE**. Jesus knew her life needed to be changed. He knew she just needed a chance at a new life. Scripture teaches that after she realized Jesus would accept her and give her what she was looking for, she left her water jug, ran to town, and began sharing with everyone what had happened.

This is an example of what is known as *repentance*. It is where a person has a change of their heart, mind, and will, and they choose to follow the will of God. You see, no one is irredeemable. Through the power of God, anyone can change. Anyone can put their faults, sins, and past failures behind them and start a new life in Christ.

Are you willing to accept that Jesus has the power to change your spouse? Do you believe that Jesus has the power to change *you*? Have you asked him to come into your heart and life and change you? Has there ever been a time when *you* "repented?"

The Bible says in Romans 3:23, "For all have sinned, and fallen short of the glory of God." And in Romans 6:23, "For the wages of sin is death; but the gift of God is eternal life through Jesus Christ our Lord." Obviously, we all need a change, and Jesus has the power to change us, but we must first ask Him to do that. Romans 10:9 says, "that if you confess with your mouth Jesus as Lord, and believe in your heart that God raised Him from the dead, you will be saved."

Jesus forgave and accepted the woman at the well, and He wants to do the same thing for you and your spouse. He has the power to change. He can redeem your marriage and even redeem your life. Will you let him?

 — Taking a Minute for Your Marriage

If you were driving on a road trip and only looked in the rearview mirror the entire way, you certainly wouldn't make it to your

destination. In fact, you would probably crash or give up at some point. Unfortunately, holding your spouse's past against them is exactly like this. The Bible says to forget what lies behind you.

When we carry hurts from the past in our hearts, we cannot make room for new happiness. Give God the pain in your marriage today so you can open your heart up to something new. Forgive your spouse for past offenses, pain, and the harm they have brought into your relationship. Make a conscious effort to let them go so you can move forward.

CHAPTER 23

TRANSPLANT "R" RESPONSIBILITY

WE LIVE IN A TIME when taking responsibility for actions and results is uncommon. Most of the time, we like to have someone else do what needs to be done, and then we blame them if the results aren't what was desired. Many times in marriage, the concept of responsibility is hard to grasp. We have to adjust to having someone around every day. We are forced to accept that we can no longer make decisions based solely on our wants and desires because there is someone else to now think about. So what do we take responsibility for, and how do we do this in our marriages?

The first way is we **HELP WITH THEIR BURDENS.** The book of Galatians instructs us to:

Bear one another's burdens, and so fulfill the law of Christ.

GALATIANS 6:2

Your spouse needs you to show compassion. They need you to hurt when they hurt. You are your spouse's helpmate. And they need to know you care about them enough to listen to what they're going through and help them deal with it! The last part of the above verse says that we fulfill the law of Christ by doing this. When we take the focus off of ourselves and seek to alleviate our spouses' burdens, we do what Jesus did and show them they're loved.

Secondly, we should **HELP WITH THEIR BETTERMENT.** In Matthew 5:13-14, Jesus calls those who follow Him salt and light. These are two things that make other things better. Throughout history, salt has been used for food preservation and flavor, antiseptic for wounds, and even payment for services rendered.

Light makes life easier. It can help reduce fear or uneasiness by causing darkness to flee so we can see clearly. Lightbulbs have even been used to refer to a moment when someone comes up with an idea or figures something out.

These two things make life easier and better. Do you do this for your marriage? We have friends who daily ask each other, "How can I make your day better?" This is awesome! How different would our relationship be if we all asked our spouses this and sought to improve their days?

This will take sacrifice and a determination to not get caught up in our own little world. Is your marriage better because of you? Do you make your spouse better by working to become better yourself? Or has your marriage lost its salt? Its flavor? Its light?

...ask each other, "How can I make your day better?"

You can become salt again to your spouse by helping around the house with nothing expected in return. Light will shine in your marriage by seeking to make your spouse and home better than it was the day before.

The third way to assume responsibility is to **HELP THEM WITH THEIR BELIEF.** Your spouse needs to believe in your belief in them. They need to believe in your marriage. Hebrews 13:4 states that marriage should be honored by all, and the marriage bed should be undefiled. Your spouse needs to trust that nothing or no one will destroy or defile your marriage through what you say and do. They need to believe your marriage is of utmost importance to you.

Your spouse should never believe that someone else or something else has your eye or heart. This may mean you cut some things out of your schedule or limit your association with certain people to help support their trust. Your spouse must know you still love them and are committed to them.

Ultimately, your marriage is your responsibility. If you commit to helping with your spouse's burdens, betterment, and beliefs, you will experience a wonderful marriage. Don't shirk your responsibility. Work at it. It's not just about you. You're in a partnership, and both of you are responsible for how it turns out!

 — *Taking a Minute for Your Marriage*

How different would your marriage be if the first thing on your mind when you woke up each day was, "How can I make his/her day better?"

What have you got to lose with this mentality? Give it a try for one week. Talk with them every morning about something you can do to help make their day go well. See if you notice a difference in the attitude, confidence, and trust your partner has toward you after working on this!

CHAPTER 24

TRANSPLANT "T" TERRITORY

TERRITORIES ARE important. Wars occur when one country invades the boundaries of another. "No Trespassing" signs are placed on property because the owners want their territory secured and protected. Have you ever thought about how your marriage has territorial borders that need protection?

Your marriage is a territory. Sadly, many couples will protect their property and possessions and not their marriages. These things we spend time trying to protect will eventually erode and disappear. But our marriages will last a lifetime if we protect them. In this chapter, let's discuss how to protect the territory of marriage by looking at a verse of Scripture that we previously used, Hebrews 13:4.

> *Let marriage be held in honor among all, and let the*
> *marriage bed be undefiled, for God will judge the*
> *sexually immoral and adulterous.*
> HEBREWS 13:4

This verse teaches that marriage should be held in honor and that the marriage bed should be undefiled (pure) because God will judge the sexually immoral and adulterous. We can make several observations about the territory of marriage. And when applied, each can help protect our marriage from vicious attacks against it.

PUTTING UP A "NO TRESPASSING" SIGN

First, we must **RESPECT THE INSTITUTION.** This verse says that marriage should be honored by all. It's not just another relationship. Marriage isn't to be taken lightly. Aside from a relationship with God, there's no other relationship worth more honor and attention than the one between a man and woman united in marriage.

Marriage has become cheapened in our world today. People choose to live together or date without ever getting married. Kids, careers, friends, and other entities take precedence over marriage. So why should there be such honor and value placed on it? Quite simply, it's the foundational relationship that God created for mankind.

The earthly institution of marriage also serves as a picture of the relationship God wants and has with Christians. Followers of Christ are referred to as "The Bride of Christ." When our marriages are honored, our spouses will feel important, and our relationship will thrive. Does your spouse feel more important than your kids, job, or friends? Would your spouse say you place a high value on your marital relationship? If not, what needs to change?

Would your spouse say you place a high value on your marital relationship?

Secondly, we must **REVERE THE INTIMACY.** In the Hebrews passage, we are instructed that the marriage bed must be undefiled or kept pure. Therefore, the territory of your marriage should have "No Trespassing" signs posted everywhere. No one should be allowed to infiltrate the intimate confines of your marriage.

Emotional attachments to someone other than your spouse are wrong. They are off-limits and should be prohibited from destroying your marriage. Satan wants you to believe that the grass is greener on the other side of the fence. He wants you to think you would be happier and more satisfied with someone else.

The truth is that the emotional, spiritual, and physical satisfaction you desire will be found only in marriage. That's the way God intended it. In Matthew 19:6, as well as Mark 10:9, Jesus states that "what God has joined together, let no man separate."

Hold firm to the intimacy of your marriage. Don't neglect physical intimacy with your spouse. God designed sex and physical intimacy to be reserved for marriage and that alone. Do not let things like pornographic websites, movies, or other vices get the attention God planned for your spouse to receive. If you are single, boyfriends and girlfriends do not get spousal privileges.

Finally, this verse teaches us to **REALIZE THE IMPACT** that comes when we violate God's plan for marriage. It says He will *judge* the adulterous and immoral. When we don't honor our marriages by respecting the institution and revering the intimacy, we can succumb to giving what's intended for our spouse to others. Understand the ramifications of this!

Many people experience pain, heartache, and psychological damage due to affairs and other destructive situations intruding on their marriage's territory. As a result, families can be torn apart. God is a loving Father, but just as a good, loving father disciplines his child, the Lord will allow us to experience pain and consequences for living outside His marriage plan. When we violate the territorial boundaries of our marriage, there will be ramifications.

The good news is that forgiveness and restoration are available. But in many cases, it comes after the damage has already been done. You can experience a meaningful, happy marriage without the pain and agony of regret from violating God's plan. Decide today that you will protect the territory of your marriage and not let anyone or anything trespass on it.

— Taking a Minute for Your Marriage

Fidelity is the quality of being loyal to someone. It stems from the Latin root "fides," meaning faith. As Christians, bound in the covenant of marriage, we must recognize that God is the author and giver of faith. Without Him as the center of our marriage, it becomes difficult to remain consistently faithful to our spouse.

Are their boundaries set within your relationship? Do you protect your marriage at all costs? If you cannot answer these questions definitively, then right now, ask the Lord to help cover you and your spouse with whatever it takes to keep your marriage your number one priority.

SECTION 6

HAVING CERTAIN-"T" IN YOUR MARRIAGE

CHAPTER 25

TEMPTATION #1 DOUBTING GOD'S WORD TO US

IN THE SECOND CHAPTER OF Genesis 2, we read that God instituted marriage between Adam and Eve. It began when Adam was placed in The Garden of Eden and was tasked with naming all animals. Scripture says there was no "suitable companion" for Adam. So God caused Adam to sleep and removed a rib from him, which He used to create Eve. From there, God presented Eve as a wife to Adam, and their marriage was established. Then God laid out a plan to ensure that Adam and Eve had His blessing and that their marriage would prosper.

God tells Adam *not* to eat from the tree of the knowledge of good and evil. God said, "All these other trees are good for you to eat. But steer clear of this one!" The fruit of all other trees in the garden was free game. Seems easy enough, right?

However, we read in Chapter 3 that there is an enemy, Satan, who seeks to destroy our marriages and families by tempting us. And he was right there, ready to bring temptation to Adam and his wife, Eve.

THE ENEMY WANTS US TO MISS GOD'S BEST FRUIT

The first way Satan tempts us is to **DOUBT GOD'S WORD!** In Genesis 3:1-3 we read that Satan, our enemy, disguised himself as a snake and slithered up to the newly married couple, where a conversation unfolded. The snake planted doubt in Eve by questioning whether God said she and Adam couldn't eat from *all* the trees in the Garden.

Eve responds with only part of what God said, including the judgment that would ensue because of disobedience. However, she even went a step further in verse 3 by adding the notion that they couldn't even *touch* the tree, let alone eat from it. So she added to what God said.

People often do this. We think we need to add to or take away parts of God's word that don't feel good to us. We doubt that what He says is enough, or maybe we think He doesn't understand our particular situation.

What God says matters! When we obey His Word and do what it says, blessing and peace come. However, when we reject what He says or add and subtract from it, we experience misery and chaos!

> *What God says matters!*

To know what God says, we must spend time with Him. Your spouse wants your time, and so does God. Make time daily to read and study a translation of The Bible you can understand. Access to Bibles is easy because there are scores of them electronically and in print. Find one that works for you and begin reading it. To start, try a chapter a day from the book of Proverbs (*which incidentally has 31 chapters—one for each day*), along with the Gospel of John.

Another crucial avenue to hearing and knowing God's word is to become active in a church. By consistently attending and serving in a church, you will find that God will lead, guide, and direct you in what He desires you to do! Those that have a hard time knowing what He says are the ones that usually don't spend time with Him reading the Bible, going to church, or in prayer.

In today's world, prayer has been relegated to times of crisis, meal times, and as a last resort when nothing else works. However, prayer was designed to be constant communication between God and us! We shouldn't just be talking and sharing our wants but also listening and responding with repentance and obedience. All throughout Scripture, we see that prayer was used in times of rejoicing and sadness. It was used as a way to hear directly from God about a decision to make. By and large, it was a top option of ways to hear from Him!

Maybe marriages today experience trouble and don't thrive as God intended because we doubt His Word. A lack of quality time with Him through the various avenues listed above is the chief reason we doubt. The lies of the world also factor in. We want things to be easy and pain-free. God never promises that to us until we get to Heaven. This thinking has caused many in our society to run and quit when things get tough. Instead, we must believe His Word as it says in Matthew 19, "Nothing should separate what He's joined together."

Never doubt what He says; do what He says! Believe His Word and watch your marriage thrive!

 — Taking a Minute for Your Marriage

Doubt is like a seed. It has to be planted to grow. Satan's primary job is to plant seeds of doubt in your mind, particularly concerning God's promises for you. When the Lord joined Adam and Eve, He gave them everything they needed for safety and blessing.

God's promise still holds for you and your spouse. But there may be seeds of doubt growing in your mind. Clear your thoughts of any hesitation or misgivings about what He has for you. Your spouse is

His gift—a suitable companion—just for you. Pause now and thank Him for his provision and blessings on your marriage.

CHAPTER 26

TEMPTATION #2 DOUBTING GOD WANTS GOOD THINGS FOR US

CONTINUING OUR LOOK at the attack of Satan on marriage in Genesis 3, we see that Satan used another tactic to destroy Adam and Eve and their marriage! In Chapter 3:4-6, Satan lies to the couple and tries to convince them that God is holding out on them, that He is a cosmic killjoy that is only out to enact judgment and pain when they mess up.

Satan does the same with us today. He wants us to believe that God is out to get us. He wants you to think that God doesn't care about you or your marriage. Buying into this lie causes pain because we seek to find the happiness and the "good things" we desire elsewhere. Satan craftily uses specific means to lure us into doubting God's desire to bless us and give us good things for us and our marriages.

First, Satan wants us to question and doubt **GOD AS A PERSON!** How we view God is crucial to everything. A. W. Tozer remarks: "What comes into our minds when we think about God is the most important thing about us." Our views and thoughts on God literally shape what we do and how we live.

If we view Him as an Almighty, omnipotent God who created all things and can save us for eternity, then He can be trusted in all other areas as well. However, when times get tough, we start stressing and allow anxious thoughts to take over. We may rush into decisions instead of seeking God's will and plan for our lives and marriage. Therefore, we must go back to the foundational truths we know about God. Trust Him that He knows all things. He sees all things. And He can do anything! Nothing is impossible for Him. He is God!

Our views and thoughts on God literally shape what we do and how we live.

Next, our enemy wants us to doubt **GOD'S PROVISION.** Satan challenges Adam and Eve by saying God didn't want them to eat from the tree because they would be like Him. In other words, he was saying, "God doesn't care about you and only cares about Himself!" But nothing could be further from the truth!

Throughout Scripture, even in this particular passage, we see that God wants to bless and provide for us. The problem is that when we violate His plan and standards, we receive brokenness and despair instead of a blessing. Adam and Eve would have experienced paradise and perfection if they hadn't bought into the lie that God didn't care for them and wouldn't take care of them.

Maybe instead of trusting that God wants to bless your marriage, you've bought into the lie to take matters into your own hands and leave—calling it quits because things are hard. God promises He will provide what we need for the hard times. Are you listening to the enemy? This will only lead to pain and agony.

Finally, Satan wants us to doubt **GOD'S PASSION FOR YOU.** After Adam and Eve ate the fruit, they began to feel overwhelming shame, regret, and the pain of the separation from God that sin causes. Verse 8 describes how they hear The Lord walking in the garden. God knew what they had done, and He came to restore their relationship that had been fractured by sin.

God loved them so much that after they experienced the consequences of their sin, He provided them with animal skins as clothing. He shed an animal's blood to cover them. This is a picture of what Jesus did for us when He died on the cross for *our* sins. God loves you and your spouse. He's passionate about your marriage and cares deeply about what happens in it. He's always available and accessible to help you and your marriage. Never doubt it!

 — Taking a Minute for Your Marriage

*Three concepts were discussed in this chapter: the **personhood** of God, the **provision** of God, and the **passion** of God. Which of these spoke to you most?*

Do you need a friend who knows and understands you fully? The Bible says that we are "friends" of God. Do you lack resources like land, food, or shelter? God is Jehovah-Jireh, the Lord, our provider. Has the fire gone out in your life because of an overfocus on yourself rather than others? The spark to reignite that fire is God's passion and glory.

Never doubt that God will supply everything you need for good times and hard times.

CHAPTER 27

TRANSACTIONAL MARRIAGE

EVERYDAY transactions happen. Banks, retail establishments, restaurants, etc., conduct their business in a transactional manner. There is a service rendered and a fee paid for the service; thus, a transaction occurs. Marriage can often become transactional because we get so busy doing things for one another that we fail to enjoy and relish the relationship itself.

We believe God desires marriage to be impactful and transformational rather than transactional. Of course, this process requires work, but it can be done. Mainly if we apply the principles shared in Luke 17: 11-19. As we read below:

> *On the way to Jerusalem he was passing along between Samaria and Galilee. And as he entered a village, he was met by ten lepers, who stood at a distance and lifted up their voices, saying, "Jesus, Master, have mercy on us." When he saw them he said to them, "Go and show yourselves to the priests." And as they went they were cleansed. Then one of them, when he saw that he was healed, turned back, praising God with a loud voice; and he fell on his face at Jesus' feet, giving him thanks. Now he was a Samaritan. Then Jesus*

> *answered, "Were not ten cleansed? Where are the nine? Was no one found to return and give praise to God except this foreigner?" And he said to him, "Rise and go your way; your faith has made you well."*
>
> LUKE 17:11-19

In this passage, we see an interesting interaction take place. Jesus is traveling and comes in contact with 10 lepers. These men suffered from a horrific skin condition that made them susceptible to labeling and ostracism from others, especially Jewish people. The lepers couldn't enter a temple to worship. They were exiled outside the city and could not communicate or come close to others, even their own families.

As the story unfolds, we see that as they encounter Jesus, they request help. They want Him to do something for them. So he tells them to go show themselves to the priests, and verse 14 says they were healed while they were on their way. But only one returned and thanked Jesus. One out of 10! Why? Because the others got what they wanted, and a transaction occurred. So what can we glean from this story to ensure our marriages aren't transactional like a business?

Only one returned and thanked Jesus.

First, we must **REMEMBER WHAT LIFE WAS LIKE BEFORE.** The leper who returned remembered what it was like to have people shun him. Thoughts of people running away from him and his inability to have normalcy likely flooded his mind. The same is true of marriage. Remember what it was like when you *weren't* married?

Maybe you were lonely. Perhaps you felt like it would never happen. Maybe you were like this man—a Samaritan and an outcast with no one to care for him. Remember how things were *before* you were married, and use those thoughts to be grateful for your marriage.

Secondly, we must **REALIZE WHAT WE GET.** This guy was so excited he literally screamed praises and threw himself at the feet of Jesus, who had given him just what he needed. He had been made whole.

When God blessed you with your spouse, He gave you exactly what you needed. A life partner. A companion to confide in. Someone to have and to hold when times are good and when times are bad. You are no longer navigating life alone; you have each other.

Finally, this story shows us that we must **RESPOND TO THE BLESSING.** The men were healed when they acted on Jesus' instruction. The one who gave thanks responded by *thanking Jesus.* When was the last time you thanked Jesus for how your life is today compared to how it used to be? Are you thankful for what you have in your marriage and for your spouse? Or do you constantly complain and harp about what you don't have or what they're not doing?

The healed man also responded by *taking action.* All the men went to the priests, but we can also infer that only this one man did what Jesus said in verse 19, "rise and go." Jesus called him to action.

To ensure our marriages aren't transactional, we must put in work. We need to take action and fiercely love and serve our spouses—not to get something in return, but because we're grateful to have them.

The man also responded by *trusting Jesus.* Jesus told him his faith had made Him well. We can trust Him with our marriages because He gave them to us. If you're single, you can trust that He will provide you a spouse and what you need.

The nine men who moved on without thanking Jesus viewed their healing as a transaction. They did what Jesus asked, and they were healed. It was an exchange of *this* for *that.*

But the one man who returned understood that there was more for him. So maybe your marriage will be healed like the leper when you apply more trust in Jesus. If He can change the lives of ten men considered inferior, diseased, and broken, He can change your marriage!

Like the grateful one, allow him to take your marriage from transactional to transformational. Agree that you will not be one of the nine who forgot to acknowledge what He had done!

 — Taking a Minute for Your Marriage

Marriage isn't a contract between two people. It is a covenant between you, your spouse, and God. It is more than just an agreement that you will remain together. It is a promise before God to stay together during the good times and in times of difficulty.

Today reaffirm your covenant and commitment to each other. Then, with your spouse in hand, recite once again the solemn vows you made before God at your wedding:

> I [   ] take thee [   ] to be my [wife/husband]. To have and to hold from this day forward, for better, for worse, for richer, for poorer, in sickness and in health, to love and to cherish until death do us part. This is my solemn vow. In Jesus' name. Amen.

SECTION 7

HOW TO KEEP YOUR MARRIAGE FROM SLIPPING

CHAPTER 28

TENSION IN MARRIAGE

WARNING SIGNS are common in the world. Advertisements are filled with medicines for anything and everything. And with these medicines come warnings of hazardous side effects, including hospitalization and death. For years, parents have warned children about sticking their fingers in electrical sockets or putting their hands on a hot stove. What if there were warnings about causes of tension, disagreements, and problems that can arise in marriage? There are!

The Bible speaks specifically to this. The book of James cuts to the chase and states that the root cause of our tension is threefold.

> *What causes quarrels and what causes fights among you? Is it not this, that your passions are at war within you? You desire and do not have, so you murder. You covet and cannot obtain, so you fight and quarrel. You do not have, because you do not ask. You ask and do not receive, because you ask wrongly, to spend it on your passions.*
> JAMES 4:1-3

The first cause is our **WARRING INWARD DESIRES.** Verse 1 says these desires battle within us. How often do we seek to be right above all else in marriage? We often belabor a point or shun our mates until they give us what we want. In your discussions, are you giving your spouse a chance to share their side of the story, or

Your desire to acquire has gone haywire!

are you adamant that you are always correct and they need to come over to your side? Is your desire to be right blurring your vision of the situation? Maybe a point of contention in your marriage is that "your desire to acquire has gone haywire!" These inward desires, based primarily on selfishness, battle against us and can leave a

path of destruction as most wars do.

The second cause of tension is the **WAY WE INTERACT WITH OTHERS.** We're told that the desires mentioned above create tension in how we deal with others. Often we verbally attack our spouses when things don't go our way, or we don't get what we want.

Verse 2 says we murder and quarrel and fight. We may not physically harm our spouse, but we can angrily snap at them, treat them with contempt, or allow hatred and discord to fester until it spews out like a volcano. Maybe your marriage is struggling and isn't what you dreamed it would be. Perhaps your spouse didn't help you with a project like they said they would. Whatever the issue is, how you handle it says a lot about you and how much your marriage means to you.

How do you interact with your spouse when things don't go your way? Do they feel murdered (destroyed) by you, your words, or your attitude? Maybe your interaction with your spouse is a problem because instead of asking God to help, you try to handle it in your own way. And instead of showing forgiveness and mercy, you feel entitled to be angry and vindictive.

James addresses the final source of tension in a marriage in this chapter: **WRONG INTENTIONS.** Verse 3 states that our motives or intentions are flawed and hinder us from enjoying the marriage and life we desire. Rather than asking Him to help us so He can be glorified and seen by others, we ask Him to change our spouse or situation so we can be happy and not be the first to apologize.

The intention of our asking goes from reconciliation with our spouse and glorification of God to self-gratification and appeasement. The underlying desire is to get *our* way rather than allow God and our spouse to have *theirs.* Selfishness matters more than unity and peace!

To have a marriage that is filled less with tension and filled more with joy, we must make sure that our inward desires are kept in check so that the way we interact with our spouses is pleasant. We also need to focus on the intentions, ensuring they aren't ruled by selfishness and self-centeredness! Imagine how different marriages (and life, in general) would be if tension was limited because we seek less of ourselves.

⧗ — *Taking a Minute for Your Marriage*

Tension occurs when something or someone is stretched tightly. An outside force is applied, and the strain causes it to give. In a marriage, pressure can stem from many different things, including incorrect words, poor actions, or even wrong intentions. You may recall a time when you had the right idea but went about it the wrong way. And sure enough, it caused tension in your relationship.

The way to relieve this is by removing the pressure. Reframe your conversation when you feel your spouse clamming up. Relax your body when your actions seem to cause them to bristle. Apologize when your best idea just went south. Keep the lines of communication open to relieve the stress and conflict in your marriage. And allow the Holy Spirit to provide warning signs to heed when there is friction within your home.

CHAPTER 29

TRACTION IN MARRIAGE – PRIORITIZING OUR SPOUSE AND THEIR FEELINGS

HAVE YOU EVER lost your footing and slipped? Or been in a vehicle trying to get over rugged terrain? The thing that is needed in both of these situations is traction. Traction keeps slippage from happening. When traction is lost, slipping and sliding occur, and damage and pain ensue in many cases. Marriages can slip and slide like vehicles and people when traction is lost.

We can do things to maintain traction in marriage and keep them from slipping and sliding into painful situations. In this section, we'll discuss three safeguards and how applying each can keep our marriages from slipping and sliding into agony, destruction, and unnecessary pain.

KEEPING YOUR SPOUSE NUMBER ONE!

The first safeguard to use is *prioritizing our spouses and their feelings*. Doing this requires us to take the focus off of ourselves and make our spouse a top priority—concerning their feelings, wants, and desires. Philippians Chapter 2 gives us a blueprint for accomplishing this.

> *Do nothing from selfish ambition or conceit, but in humility count others more significant than yourselves. Let each of you look not only to his own interests, but also to the interests of others.*
> PHILIPPIANS 2:3-4 ESV

To start, we must **OPT FOR SELFLESSNESS OVER SELFISHNESS**. We are challenged in verse 3 to do nothing out of selfishness. This totally flips the script on everything the world around us says. Our culture is plagued with entitlement and narcissism. We are consumed with the "what's in it for me" mentality. Even marriages fall prey to this, and many meet their demise because of selfishness and the "me over we" attitude.

Secondly, we keep our marriage traction stable by being **OTHERS FOCUSED.** The barometer for this is made clear in these verses. When we focus on our spouse more than ourselves, we will see great things happen in our marriages. And it requires humility.

Immediately following the topic of selfishness, Paul encourages us to be humble. This word is often misconstrued. Many think humility involves weakness or a low self-image. In actuality, humility is the opposite. It's strong confidence. Humility is not thinking less of yourself but thinking about yourself less.

In your marriage, do you constantly think about Y-O-U and your desires? Do you only do things for your spouse when asked or for a special occasion? When humility is present, no fanfare or accolades are needed to validate efforts and intentions. So Paul starts the discussion on self-centeredness by talking about humility. Because, without humility, no relationship—especially marriage, will thrive.

After humility, the next step to becoming more focused on others is to *see them properly*. Verse 3 continues by challenging us to consider others more significant than ourselves. This goes hand-in-hand with Jesus' teaching on the second greatest commandment: to love others as we love ourselves.

If we're honest, we love ourselves a lot! We constantly need reminders that the world doesn't revolve around us. In marriage, it's not just you. A partner needs to feel special, loved, and meaningful. Does your spouse feel important? Do they think they're more important to you than your schedule, friends, or hobbies? If we place more emphasis on making our spouses feel important, wanted, and needed, our marriages will flourish.

> *A partner needs to feel special, loved, and meaningful.*

The final key to prioritizing our spouses and their feelings is to *show interest in what interests them*. Verse 4 concludes by encouraging us not to simply focus on what interests us but on what interests others. "Look out for" in the original language means to "fix our eyes upon."

When was the last time you didn't just boringly sit through an activity that interested your spouse but instead you really looked into it? Do you know why they have a particular interest? Do you know what interests them at all?

Maybe what your marriage needs is for your spouse to feel like you are interested in what makes them tick and why. E.g., Why do they watch the shows they watch? Why do they like the team they follow? Do you know? Does your spouse feel like you care?

The key to success in marriage is to prioritize your spouse. Make sure they know they're important to you, and your marriage will thrive. If they feel unimportant, your relationship may struggle to survive!

— Taking a Minute for Your Marriage

Dale Carnegie said, "You can make more friends in two months by becoming interested in other people than you can in two years by trying to get other people interested in you." Likewise, marriage counselors often say that the best marriages begin as friendships.

Commit the next 60 days to becoming a better friend with your spouse by showing great interest in what interests them. The results will likely be amazing! One suggestion is to plan a surprise date night with them. Go above and beyond to research their interests and do something that shows they are important to you and that you value their interests.

CHAPTER 30

TRACTION IN MARRIAGE – MINIMIZE OUR SPOUSE'S FAULTS

AS WE CONTINUE at ways to keep our marriages from slipping and sliding into crevices of danger and destruction, we come to a topic that is easy to talk about when it's focusing on others. But it is also something we don't want to deal with when confronted with it personally. The topic is *faults*.

In marriage, this topic is played out in the "blame game." We focus on what our spouse does wrong and minimize our faults. Unfortunately, the blame game and words like "you always" or "you never" characterize many marriages that are dangerously close to slipping off potential cliffs into trouble because minimizing our spouses' faults is not the norm.

We can change this, however, by taking lessons from a story in the book of John, Chapter 8. In this story, a woman caught in the act of adultery is brought by religious leaders before Jesus to test His reaction, discredit His teaching, and shame her. Instead, everything changes. Verses 1-6 set the stage, and then beginning in verse 7, Jesus gives responses that we can use to help our marriages gain and keep traction.

> *But Jesus went to the Mount of Olives. Early in the morning he came again to the temple. All the people came to him, and he sat down and taught them. The scribes and the Pharisees brought a woman who had been caught in adultery, and placing her in the midst they said to him, "Teacher, this woman has been caught in the act of adultery. Now in the Law, Moses commanded us to stone such women. So what do you say?" This they said to test him, that they might have some charge to bring against him. Jesus bent down and wrote with his finger on the ground. And as they continued to ask him, he stood up and said to them, "Let him who is without sin among you be the first to throw a stone at her."*
>
> JOHN 8:1-7

First, Jesus reminds them that **FAULTS ARE COMMON IN EVERYONE.** He tells them that "anyone who is sinless can cast a stone at her." In other words, no one aside from Jesus is perfect. You and your spouse will mess up. Cut each other some slack.

If you read on to verse 9, it says, "But when they heard it, they went away one by one, beginning with the older ones, and Jesus was left alone with the woman standing before Him." The Pharisees realized that everyone has faults, and therefore they had no right to condemn her

Chances are your spouse already knows they messed up. They may even be trying to correct their wrongs. So, the last thing they need is to hear you acting as if you are perfect and railing on their imperfections. Instead, be humble and honest, responding in a way that shows you understand what it's like to be imperfect. Their mess is no reason for you to give up on them or your marriage.

The second teaching we see here is that **FORGIVENESS ALWAYS TRUMPS CONDEMNATION.** If you read on, verses

10-11 show a beautiful picture of restoration, love, and a willingness to look past the action to see the person.

After Jesus engages her with a question about where her accusers are, she tells Him they are gone. Jesus then tells her that He doesn't condemn her either and challenges her to use this act of forgiveness to change her life! Your spouse needs your compassion, not your condemnation.

Forgiveness can't happen until compassion is present. Just as Jesus saw the woman as more valuable than her faults, we must also see our spouses that way. I'm sure there are times when your spouse has forgiven you for harsh words, selfishness, and many other things. Therefore, you can forgive them and show compassion. Will you do that for your spouse? Forgiveness trumps condemnation.

Your spouse needs your compassion, not your condemnation.

If there is bitterness and unforgiveness in your marriage, let it go. Everyone makes mistakes, and your spouse needs to know that you forgive theirs; you don't condemn them! The life and health of your marriage are at stake.

The very thing that could keep it from toppling over the edge and ending is minimizing what they *do* and maximizing who they *are.* God has given them to you! He wants you to forgive and not condemn. When you do, you point them to Jesus, who willingly forgives all of us no matter what we do or have done. Let your marriage show the world, and its condemning nature, more of Jesus and His forgiveness!

 — Taking a Minute for Your Marriage

The Proverbs teach that people are wise when they restrain their anger and overlook faults. This is to his credit. It is natural to want to point out someone's mistakes because we justify that we're simply

helping them do better. But when this happens repeatedly, it can erode a relationship.

Most mistakes aren't that major, and overlooking them is often the wiser choice. God's grace empowers us to focus on what is good in a person rather than what's wrong.

Today, when you begin to critically evaluate your husband or wife's flaws, immediately turn your attention to something positive about them. Find ten good qualities that supersede the one fault. Repeatedly doing this will shift your mind's focus to the power of God's love and away from the worldly nature of criticism.

SECTION 8

FINAL THOUGHTS & AUTHORS' COMMENTARY

CHAPTER 31

TRIUMPHANT MARRIAGE THAT WINS AND LASTS

YOU'RE ABOUT TO WIN! As you have journeyed through this book, whether daily, weekly, or once in a while, it's our prayer that you have gleaned tips and ideas applicable to your marriage. We also pray that you have come away with a greater appreciation for married couples and more profound love and gratefulness for your spouse!

We want your marriage to win! We want it to triumph against the obstacles, struggles, and attacks the world throws at it. So to conclude, we offer a couple of reminders you can use from here on out to have a triumphant marriage that lasts until death do you part. We often refer back to these reminders as we observe other couples whose marriages have stood the test of time. So now let's go win.

Reminder #1: A triumphant lifelong marriage is possible.
Multiple times in the Scriptures, we are told that with God, *all* things are possible. When a thought is repeated over and over in Scripture, it shows how emphatic God is that we understand it. All things are possible with God! When God says "all," we can't replace

it with "some!" Your marriage is part of *all things*! And your marriage can last! You can make it!

For Jesus to repeat this five times shows how emphatic He is that we understand it is possible. Including God in your marriage increases the likelihood of making it because His power is strong enough to sustain you and help you persevere!

Reminder #2: A triumphant lifelong marriage is powerful.

Have you ever seen a couple whose marriage is one you admire? It could be they've been married for a long time, and that example inspires you. Our marriages can be warnings, or they can be examples. We can warn others of what *not* to do. Or we can be a model of what *to* do.

Titus 2:8 states, "Your message is to be sound beyond reproach so that any opponent will be ashamed because he doesn't have anything bad to say." Your marriage can be like this. It can be such an example that no one can say anything bad about it. How you talk to and about your spouse, how you love and serve them, and your commitment to stay with and fight for them all serve as a pattern others can use to follow.

Reminder #3: A triumphant lifelong marriage can be a portrait of true love.

When marriages endure storms and trials, it shows the depth and magnitude of love. The most famous verse in The Bible, John 3:16, states that God loved you and me so much that He gave His One and Only Son, Jesus, for the payment of our sin penalty. The ultimate sign of love is giving. Marriages that last are ones in which both spouses consistently give themselves for the other.

Demonstrating high regard for your marriage to your spouse and others may save it from divorce. Your spouse will know you love them and are committed to the long haul when they feel valued. Is the portrait your marriage paints one of love? Or are you painting a picture of hostility, discouragement, and giving up?

Others are observing the representation of your marriage. The question is, what are they seeing? Love is shown through giving. Give to your spouse, give to your marriage. Be a giver, not a getter. Honestly, we give so much to so many other people and things. It's time to give to our marriages.

AUTHORS' COMMENTARY

Thank you for taking the time to read this book. Your marriage is important to us and, most importantly, to God. We pray that as you grow closer to each other by applying these principles, you will grow closer to God!

Remember, He created marriage. He gave (or will give) your spouse to you and wants you to cherish that gift—not waste it or take it for granted. Your marriage can soar and thrive.

We encourage you to go back and revisit these pages often, taking a few minutes to give your marriage a tune-up or even an overhaul. Join us from this day forward, for better or worse, in sickness and in health, to work on your marriage and stay the course until death do you part. You can do this by focusing on your spouse and marriage one minute at a time.

We also urge you to supplement the teachings in this book by watching our daily videos or attending one of our marriage conferences. Obtain more information about these at www.thewordministries.net. Or follow us on Facebook, TikTok, or Instagram by searching for Minute4Marriage or The WORD Ministries.

ABOUT THE AUTHORS

JON AND TERESA HARPER have been married for over 25 years. Though one is a product of divorced parents, and the other witnessed a marriage that lasted over 48 years, they have each committed to making their marriage work for a lifetime. Through struggles, joys, highs, and lows, Jon and Teresa continue to navigate life together and seek to help others build marriages that will last forever.

The Harpers believe that marriage is a gift and should be treated as such. Their own commitment to the sanctity of marriage propels them to want to help others on their journey.

Jon and Teresa have been in ministry for 25 years, traveling and speaking to groups throughout the US for the last 14 years. Their passion for the Lord has given them opportunities to speak at various conferences, retreats, weekend events, and crusades to thousands of people. The Harpers reside in Texas and are the proud parents of three children and one son-in-law!

To learn more about the Harpers, visit their website: thewordministries.net.

Made in USA - Kendallville, IN
22495_9781737356776
01.13.2023 1341